Waiting on Deros

A Soldier's Story

Adrian Falchion
Floyd Odekirk

ISBN-978-0-9818974-8-6
LCCNumber: 2012949348

Waiting on DEROS: A Soldier's Story could not have been accomplished without the efforts of a Veteran, a writer and the spirit of every soldier walking within the pages of this book. Floyd Odekirk pursued the emotional task of bringing back the images of his tour in Vietnam (1968-69) so that the writer, Adrian Falchion, could paint in all its vibrant and dark colors the truths of war.

Following the completion of 19 stories, Floyd Odekirk offered the light to his Veteran Brothers Michael Bennett, David Higgins, Craig Johnson, Dale Moravec, Donald Burch, Patrick Callahan, Joseph DeAugustine, Robert Moneypenny, Daniel Michael Pruitt and Thomas Vojvodich who each shared a story for the sake of honoring other soldiers.

The 25 stories included within this book were written with an accuracy only deflected by the elapse of time, the faltering of recollection and a journey which entailed for the soldiers remembering events that wanted to be forgotten.

Thank you Angels. . .for you have lit the darkness, brightened the colors and inspired the gift.

THE THINGS WE REMEMBER

The truth of war did not happen all at once. . .not like being yanked from our country and dropped into the jungle. We learned slowly, watching the soldiers who had been in Nam for awhile, even though they had already learned not to let us new guys get close.

In the beginning, when we went on patrol, a soldier named Turlington usually took point. He had been *in country* during the Tet Offensive and knew how to detect the hidden trip wires and rigged grenades. He knew how to travel through the jungle while avoiding the poisonous vipers that had been tethered within the bamboo thickets, and he had a knack for noticing the punji sticks buried beneath leaves.

He would work his way through the twisted vines and long grass, each soldier following by stepping exactly in his tracks. When he held up his fist. . .we froze.

Every night, like a ritual, Turlington sharpened his knife with a razor strap, until the blade gleamed like a cold, silver crescent moon.

We were amongst experienced men, fierce fighters, who we, in the beginning, didn't dare piss off. We watched these soldiers, because they had kept themselves alive, and we figured that they had found the secret that the dead soldiers had not known.

The truth of war did not happen all at once. We learned slowly. We thought we knew what fear felt like. We thought we knew, until green tracer rounds blasted through the blackness, and muzzle flashes from the jungle sent bullets shrilling past our helmets. We learned to calculate each rifle shot, reload, click, crack. We watched as other soldiers fell, and braced ourselves for the sharp jolt that could take us down.

We had seen the expression of other soldiers when the bullet struck, splattering red. They looked like they didn't understand how it happened, and what the hell should they do, because everyone else was being shot at, and they needed help, and they didn't want to be hauled away in a black bag.

The truth of war did not happen all at once. We thought we knew pain. We thought we knew, until we heard soldiers screaming for hours after the morphine ran out. We saw soldiers get ripped apart, tossed like riff-raff and then sprawled on the ground with splintered bones sticking through burning flesh, their blood soaking away into the earth.

We were young, afraid and innocent. . .in the beginning. We hoped that if we stepped on a mine, the explosion would kill us clean and not just blow off our legs. We took what we learned and wore the truth like worthless medals. We watched soldiers get shot, lose limbs, plead, scream and cry. We knew when the morphine ran out.

One night, back at base camp, we heard over the communications radio the panicked voice of a radio operator at the Water Point whose small troop was under attack. We thought the artillery and gun ships would help them, but quickly realized that they were not going to get any help, because both Artillery Hill and the allotment of gun ships were already elsewhere deployed.

A group of us soldiers decided to get our tanks going, but the first sergeant had his men positioned on both ends of the barracks, barricading our route. He knew that if we went, we would be ambushed, but we would have volunteered.

Instead, we went back and listened to the communications radio. The fire fight lit the ridge about three quarters of a kilometer south of Camp Enari. We watched the U.S. troop's red tracer rounds and the enemy's blasts. We saw flares fired into the darkness, a green glow that cast shifting shadows of the jungle across the sky.

The soldier on the radio pleaded for help. They were running low on ammo. The enemy was approaching. The RTO tried again. We heard the distinctive crack of the AK-47s in the background and the *whomp* of the mortars.

Then the radio went silent.

We got drunk.

We drank to forget the radio operator's voice, the other men of his troop. . .to forget for at least that night that we had stood listening as soldiers died.

We were learning.

War left no time for dwelling on death. I was the only tank mechanic of E Co. 4th Engineers, and broken tanks meant stranded soldiers surrounded by snipers. I worked morning until night, under the hot sun and in the monsoon rains, but the calls kept coming from platoons broken down and under attack.

The truth of war did not happen all at once. We learned slowly while death happened swiftly. In the beginning of my tour, when a soldier from camp got killed, I would go to the memorial service. . .felt like the decent thing to do.

Only a few guys would show up, the chapel offered a

dreary, dim light through the colored glass windows, the hymns usually drifted off key, and the chaplain appeared weary of talking about dead boys that neither he nor the God he worshiped could help.

One day, early in my tour, when I returned from a mission, a respected Specialist E-5 approached me. Three men of his crew were with him, but they had slowed their strides to keep a distance back. This Specialist E-5 glanced at the three other soldiers as if trying, with their unity, to alleviate for me the abrupt gravity of what he needed to report. He then explained that on their last bridge assignment my best friend had been killed.

I stood staring at him. . .not comprehending. . .or refusing to believe. He sympathized with my confused reaction and repeated the name.

I felt a cold emptiness while standing in 100 degree heat. I asked how it happened, only because I didn't know what else to say, and because I needed to know, needed to envision my friend's death, because that was the only thing left to give him. I wanted to feel the emotion like I had been with him, because I knew that I would eventually need to forget.

I walked away trying to understand the war, trying to understand existence, trying to understand why such a good kid got caught and killed in the middle. I blamed God, while beginning to believe that God could not exist, because my best friend had died.

I felt the disappointment and disapproval of the other guys when I decided not to attend the memorial, but like every other memorial service, the body would have already gone to Graves Registration. I didn't want to hear the hymns and prayers without my friend's body being there.

If his body had been at the chapel, I would have attended the service.

I learned that war keeps taking. I learned to lock away the emotions. I tried to forget the anguish and pain of my best friend's death, but eventually, I only forgot his name, a name that I would years later desperately try to remember.

At about four months into my tour, I knew that I was going to die in Vietnam. I stopped writing letters, lost track of time and went without sleep for days. The kid I had been before the war faded. . .an untamed soldier took his place. My friends were becoming fewer.

The truth of war did not happen all at once. We thought we understood resignation. We thought we understood, until we went into battles believing that we were only risking lives that had already been taken, and when we did not die, we wondered what was left of ourselves to bring home.

We cannot escape the Vietnam War. The shadow follows, trying to drag us back into the trenches, trying to drag us back to the truth of what we endured. We yet feel the enemy lurking in the darkness. We hear the explosions and the screams of soldiers. During the night, we see our Brothers drenched with blood. We watch life through dimmed colored glass windows. We have been changed, and we cannot go back to who we were before the war or what we once did not know. What we have tried to forget, are the very things that we remember.

DEMAND NOT THE SACRIFICE

I volunteered for the war. I was 18, looking for escape, hoping for adventure. I wanted to be infantry, rifle ready, charging the enemy, but the army had a different plan. After considerable convincing, I agreed to become a tank mechanic. I learned later that being infantry, the *grunts*, meant slopping through monsoon swamped jungles and humping in relentless heat, targets for snipers and buried mines. I began to think that, perhaps, I had been lucky.

I went to basic training at Fort Campbell. From there I was sent to Wheel & Vehicle School at Fort Dix to learn about gas engines and mechanics. My next stop would be Fort Knox. I was late for reporting, because I had been arrested for hitchhiking out of uniform.

Fort Knox trained us soldiers in track & diesel, weapons, map reading, operating military equipment and other useful things. We practiced disassembling and assembling our M-16s. We learned to be quick and accurate. Later, we learned how to assemble our M-16s in the dark.

In Jungle Training we practiced military maneuvers in simulated villages, with explosions, snipers, and guys on the ground with blown off limbs. We knew that the snipers were our own men, the guys on the ground were actually uninjured and the killing wasn't real. What did concern us, while sliding on our backs under concertina wire, were the real poisonous snakes.

Next, I was given orders for deployment to Vietnam,

with two weeks leave before reporting to Fort Lewis. Once again, I was delayed, this time by immunizations, processing and paperwork. The plane that I should have been on was forced down in Russia.

Our plane landed briefly in the Philippines, a cross path for soldiers going to Vietnam and soldiers returning back home. We watched these soldiers who had survived their tour walk past. Their uniforms were faded and filthy. Their expressions were grim and empty. We didn't understand. We felt ready.

We arrived at Cam Ranh Bay and next, Pleiku Airbase, and then took a bus to Camp Enari. There were over 100 guys already gathered for orientation and processing. The soldiers were then directed to their different units.

Not long after, a group of these soldiers geared up for patrol. These new guys, having become tough from training, appeared eager for action. They wanted to prove themselves as heroes. They strutted with bravado, while tossing back and forth claims of courage and confidence. They weren't scared. . .hell no. They strode away like they were immortal.

Not all of them survived.

The soldiers who did return, trudged through camp, a few with bloody bandages, their rifles slung over their slumped shoulders. They stared straight forward, with sweat soaked faces and grimy uniforms, and simply shook their heads when we tried to find out what had happened.

I knew then that Vietnam was not an adventure. Vietnam was about proud, defiant soldiers going on patrol and returning with broken beliefs. Vietnam was about boys going on patrol and getting killed.

We felt the cold shadow of war descending and hoped that our names would not be called. We didn't want to know what had changed the first group sent out on patrol or the soldiers with whom we had crossed paths while in the Philippines, but in the end, we all knew.

When E Company, 4th Engineers needed a mechanic, I got the job. A Sergeant took me out in an Armored Vehicle Launch Bridge tank (AVLB). The Sergeant was a career soldier, in his early twenties, with scars across his arms and face to prove his battles. The tank was powered by a 750 HP diesel engine, measured a width of 3.67 meters across and weighed 58 ton.

We took the tank towards Pleiku with only our M-16s. The Sergeant wanted to know how I would react under pressure, and had the tank going fast, grinding through the wet mud. In a lower area of the road, the months of monsoon rain had created a four foot deep incline. Our tank lurched down, the sludgy mud covering the tracks and splashing into the hatches. Once past, our tank began slowing even further because of the rise of the road.

There were Vietnamese in scooters skirting the edge of the tank trail, including a guy on a Honda 65cc motorcycle. He was wearing a baseball style hat, light colored short sleeved shirt and black pants. His shoes looked like *Ho Chi Minh slicks*.

When we got nearer, he pulled out onto our path. The Sergeant didn't slow down, and the guy on the cycle kept just out of the tank's reach.

Then our tank began gaining ground, nearly striking the rear tire of the motorcycle. The Vietnamese guy was gripping the handles, trying to control his bike in the mud.

I watched the Sergeant in an effort to understand his unexplained tactic. His expression indicated nothing, like he was playing emotional military games with a new mechanic.

Amid the rumbling of the tank, as our tracks rolled alarmingly near the cyclist, I yelled over and over again that we were going to hit him, but the Sergeant did not reply, did not react and did not slow down.

I watched the speed of our tank against the pace of the cycle. Then I tried reaching the Vietnamese guy with the sheer force of my thoughts, trying to direct his cycle clear of our tank. I desperately wanted him to get out of the way, because I knew that I couldn't go against the Sergeant.

Why the hell wasn't he getting out of the way?!

Then it became just that instant. . .the tank, the Sergeant, and the guy on the cycle. I braced myself, even while denying the inevitable, because if we hit him, crushed him, killed him, then how would I stay the same?

I wouldn't. I didn't. We hit him.

Metal crunched beneath us. The right track shifted slightly as if over an incidental rut. I knew enough about what tanks could do, and that image kept going through my thoughts. I tried to grasp reality, but the reality kept drowning me. I felt a cold current of fear. I felt unsteady. I felt like I would be sick. We had struck a guy with a 58 ton tank.

The hell with the whole damn war.

On the way back, I raged about what had happened, until the Sergeant told me to shut the hell up. Then I sat quietly, wondering if the guy was dead, wondering what I should do, because I knew that the guy had to be dead.

When we got back to camp, I told a few other soldiers. They shrugged like it didn't mean shit. I went to the officers and the other sergeants. They listened like I was an annoyance and then told me I was dismissed. I tried telling anyone who I thought could help. Eventually there was no one left to tell, so I took what I knew and locked the truth away as if it had never happened.

Only later, did I understand. The deep mud trench within near proximity to the rise of the road had provided the obstacles to slow down our tank. The cyclist had then intended to bring our tank to a complete halt, giving the Vietcong the ideal opportunity to attack.

The Sergeant had not hesitated, and his knowledge and decision had kept us alive.

War brought a different reality. . .kill or be killed, simple reckless rule. For those soldiers who thought there existed a third choice, a noble choice, they lost their lives and perhaps risked the lives of their platoons. Every soldier watched death and dealt death. We thought that war would make us heroes. We learned that war could far easier make us dead. In the end, none of us were lucky.

DEROS

Time in war promises nothing, but changes everything. Each day in Nam became like the haze of drifting red dirt. Weeks became battles lost in allusions. Months became like forgotten fragments ripping through our thoughts. A one year tour sounded easy enough, until the reality of war struck. Then time became the counting of soldiers zapped and zipped into black bags.

My battalion was part of the 4th Infantry Division, E Company, 4th Engineers. We built bridges, removed land mines, and were volunteered as tunnel rats, amongst other things. We were stationed at Camp Enari, a mile or two adjacent to the city of Pleiku.

Two months into my tour, on an August morning, I found my name on the clerk's office bulletin board roster for a *listening post,* a military operation with the purpose of observing, verifying and gaining knowledge of the enemy's number and route near our base camp.

The 40 assigned soldiers gathered up their gas masks, atropine syrettes, M-16s, a couple bandoliers of ammunition and two grenades each. We then crawled into the back of a couple of deuce and a half trucks. The trucks rumbled through the gate and down the road while we sat side by side, checking our gear and glancing about at the passing terrain.

About three miles north east, we unloaded, with rifles

aimed, our eyes darting over the land for snipers or traps, while keeping ready to hit the ground. We then hiked one behind the next for about an hour and set up a mock military position in case the enemy had us under surveillance. Even if the enemy did not have us under surveillance, we were to leave no sign that we had ever been there.

The sun sank behind a sky as black as ash, and we slowly, silently proceeded forward for another half mile, following the soldier in front of us, and prowling through the darkness like hunted wolves. Our canteens had already been emptied, so that the water did not swish while we walked. We had straightened the cotter pins in our grenades so that our defense could be quick. Our dog tags had been bound together with black electrical tape.

When we reached our location, a barren flat land with scattered bushes, we divided into two groups of 20, and once again set up our defensive perimeters. Two soldiers kept together every 20 feet around the circle, the standard procedure for overlapping field of fire.

The M-60 was propped in place on a bipod with the operating soldier on his stomach, peering through the steel sight, with another soldier positioned beside him, ready to feed in the bandolier of bullets. The rest of us sat back to back, shivering, with our cold M-16s pressed against our palms.

We waited.

The enemy came, walking lightly and dressed in black, like ominous shadows. I heard the soft metallic clinks of their weapons being hauled. I heard the Vietcong's whispering in eerie drones and hoped that the cadence of their conversation would not change.

We slowed our breathing into a forced, steady quiet,

while our hearts thumped in frantic pace. The soldier leaning against me went rigid. I could feel the tightening of his muscles against my back. He and I were only ten feet from the path.

Hour after hour the enemy walked past, easily hundreds of Vietcong. Our muscles ached, and our feet and shoulders became numb from keeping position. Every soldier knew that his life depended on every other soldier's perseverance to keep panic held down. If just one of the Vietcong caught the faintest sound or sensed our presence, as if drawn by the fixed stares beneath our helmets, we were as good as dead.

I thought about my family and what I had last said to them or did not say. I tried to remember how things had been before believing that I would be blown apart in a far off country. I thought about what I would do if a Vietcong turned my direction and aimed an AK-47 at my chest. I thought about God, and wondered...hoped that He existed, because we were sitting only ten feet away from death. I decided that if the Vietcong turned with their weapons, I would not die easy.

And then, imperceptibly, the darkness faded. With the warmth of the sun, the enemy disappeared. We had been spared. We returned to camp feeling as though we had defeated at least a stroke of time in war.

The next day, another group of boys were assigned for the listening post. A black soldier named Harris, a good guy with a pleasant smile, who had been at Camp Enari for a long time as an engineer, but had never been off the base, wanted to give his part one last time for his Brothers before going home. He was not on the list, but he searched the camp for another soldier to exchange places with him. He joined the group sent off for that night's covert mission.

27

One of the groups got hit. Maybe someone messed up. Maybe someone adjusted his weapon or slid his boot or could not keep his breathing quiet. Maybe no one messed up. Maybe the enemy just happened to notice our guys lying low, with the blackness of night being their only cover.

We heard that the RTO had called for Medevac, but the location had not been considered secure. We heard that the morphine ran out. We heard that Harris had been in the group attacked. With only one week left before his *Date Eligible for Return from Over Seas*, he had taken the place of another soldier.

Death within war waits readily and without remorse. The counting down of a soldier's one year tour in Vietnam became his only light of hope and a desperate walk through darkness as he watched other soldiers get killed. Richard Harned and Billy D. Harris lost their lives on that night and went home early as dead soldiers.

In the end, time did not make a difference, because death could happen within a soldier's first battle or in the last day of his tour. Time in war promises nothing, but changes everything.

Operation Clean Sweep

Over 2000 soldiers on that September day methodically went through their gear with whatever ritual they believed worked best against the vices of war. Soldiers from Alpha, Bravo, Charlie, Delta and Echo Company checked their weapons, sharpened their bayonets, and took apart and cleaned their M-16 bolt carriers and barrels, before putting the rifles back together, wiped free of oil and loaded with only 18 or 19 rounds in a 20 round clip, because the M-16 was notorious for jamming up when fired.

Of the impending mission, we knew the name, *Operation Clean Sweep*, but little else. Only the chopper pilots, medics, perimeter guards and the soldiers at Artillery Hill, an area of significant fire support, would stay back in camp with gates locked and rolls of concertina wire hauled into place.

Near the end of the day, I sat on a bottom bunk with a sheet of PX stationery. I wrote home about guard duty and other uneventful things like the rats and snakes. I wrote that I would be going on a mission in the morning, but not the purpose, because of security reasons, and because I didn't yet know the details. I wanted to write how much I loved my family, but the idea of including such an emotional sentiment clashed with my effort to appear courageous. I finished the letter without allowing the thought of death to distract my confidence.

That night, I lay on my back wondering about the search

and destroy mission. Cots creaked as soldiers awakened and then tried to get back to sleep.

With the morning light, we strode from our barracks and fell into formation, wearing jungle fatigues, bandoliers of bullets crisscrossed over our chests and grenades, bayonets and canteens strapped onto our belts.

A convoy of deuce and a half trucks were waiting. We loaded up, over 2000 soldiers, and drove in different directions but all within a seven mile radius of the camp. When we reached the assigned location, our group climbed down from the trucks and strung out in a line over a mile long. The operation entailed walking back to camp through the jungle, while on the lookout for any indication of the enemy.

The trees towered 100 feet high, with fanned leaves like a green tarp draped against the light. Shrubs, plants and branches became barricades that lashed at our sleeves and faces. Tangled vines ensnared our boots, shadows of poisonous vipers flicked past our vision, and the mosquitoes were nothing less than vicious.

We were supposed to stay in our linear line, but the point man had pulled a machete from his belt and began hacking through the foliage. We followed him in single file with only the sounds of the swinging blade against the stalks and our boots crushing through the deep drifts of green. After awhile, the jungle relented enough for us to return back into fanned formation.

We had walked for a few hours, our unwavering vigilance falling in rhythm with our stride, when a soldier on my right accidentally hit the trigger of his M-79. The barrel ricocheted back with a blast, shooting off an explosive round. The two soldiers walking in front, having heard the

M-79 fire and the thud of the round landing between them, halted abruptly, mid step. The guys nearby turned with alarm, while soldiers further away hit the ground.

Nothing happened.

The explosive had not tumbled enough to detonate. The two soldiers eventually took a breath, cursing while they struggled to regain their military composure. The rest of the soldiers tried to restrain the tension that appeared to zap through the line of boys like a strike of electricity.

The soldier with the M-79 stood quietly with his helmet tilted down over his glasses. He had been given the M-79 because of his poor vision, but with whatever weapon, he was not cut out for infantry. Although he couldn't fix an engine, he knew every answer for any mechanical question. He had proven to be a loyal friend, and his photographic memory made him a valuable soldier. A gun simply made him dangerous.

Craig Johnson, the radio operator from another platoon further down, radioed our RTO, wanting to know what was happening with us. Our RTO reported back to Johnson and the other troops the explanation of the blast, while we made the soldier put a shot gun round of buckshot in the M-79 grenade launcher to prevent the explosion of another accidental discharge. We knew that he would fare poorly with the short range ammo if we got caught in a fire fight, but while we weren't in battle, the rest of us felt better.

We forged onward until the point man reached a river that spanned about 20 feet across. The embankment on both sides rose almost vertical, and the water's current ran swift. Our group slowly gathered, knowing that we were standing in a perfect place to be ambushed by the enemy. We waited until a certain soldier arrived. This soldier had been a notable athlete on his high school swim team, and as he unhooked his gear, his confidence was evident.

After tying a rope around his waist, he dove in, and I hoped that the confidence he had in his ability could get him across, because the current quickly yanked him out of our sight. Nearly 15 minutes later, we finally saw him endeavoring through the tumultuous water. When he reached the other side, he tied the rope around a tree.

Each soldier then crossed the river by holding his rifle above the water in one hand, while gripping the rope with the other as the current tore against him. In the deepest parts, we had to hold our breath. We climbed the bank on the other side, our boots sloshing.

As we worked our way forward through the jungle, we could barely see 15 feet in front. We used the vines and bushes to pull ourselves up the steep slopes and then struggled to keep on our feet while sliding down the opposite side.

Eventually the terrain became more level and less vegetated. The point man, advancing with caution, noted when, with one step, his foot went down further than expected, and he abruptly halted. Using his bayonet, he swept the blade horizontally through the leaves, striking against buried punji sticks. Slowly he then worked his way across, gliding the bayonet, plotting his approach like a warrior in a perilous chess game. Each soldier followed, adjusting his pace and stance, so that he could step exactly in the foot fall of the point man. Once across, we spread back out.

The temperature was near 100 degrees that day, and after a few hours, the radio operator's stride became slow and staggered. He shifted the PRC-25 radio on his shoulder, hoping to balance the extra weight, while trying to keep alongside of the sergeant.

Sweat ran down his face and his breathing sounded rough. He didn't complain. . .just kept going until he fell over. The medic got out the water and salt, while a few of us unhooked the boy's heavy gear. The radio got passed to another soldier. A couple of the guys then hoisted the RTO back onto his feet and stayed with him until he felt able enough to walk on his own.

Our company sergeant, a soldier who had been recalled out of retirement, looked equally pale, but he kept going, never expecting anything more from his men than what he could give himself.

Instead, he took compassion on another RTO who looked like he was also struggling. The sergeant told me to take over the radio, and I didn't question him, but I didn't want that radio with an antenna over ten feet high like a silver flag pointing me out to the Vietcong. If the enemy attacked, the RTO always keeps with his sergeant, and the sergeant usually finds his way into the worst of the battle, and that thought scared the hell out of me.

We proceeded with good pace until we reached a clearing, where a bull water buffalo was charging back and forth on our path. The creature easily weighed over 2000 pounds, stood over the height of us soldiers, horns in a threatening arc, snorting and stamping the earth with challenge.

I was thinking that we were going to get ambushed by the enemy while trying to get across that clearing. I was thinking that I was going to get trampled by that bull buffalo. I was thinking that we were all going to get ambushed while I got trampled because of that damn 26 pound prick radio strapped onto my back.

A few soldiers on the far left finally distracted the buffalo enough for the rest of us to cross through. We kept going until the end of Operation Clean Sweep.

With the trucks waiting, we climbed into the backs, the weight of our gear feeling far heavier. We were grimy and itchy and our muscles ached with weariness. We sat quietly, our exhaustion rivaled by the jolting of the trucks.

On that September day, we had crossed through a wild river, while wondering if we would be ambushed on the other side. Our RTO had toppled over from heat exhaustion. If not for our intuitive point man, we would have been speared by punji sticks. We had eluded enemy traps and escaped the wrath of a riled bull water buffalo. Two thousand Camp Enari soldiers had battled through seven miles of Vietcong jungle and not one had died.

In Nam, that was considered a good day.

The Silence of War

With the haze of exhaust mixing with the heat of a high sun, the wrecker driver maneuvered around the convoy, halting alongside the skewed line of abandoned engineer dump trucks that barricaded over an eighth of a mile of road. He then directed a rookie soldier to climb out and wait.

Keeping his rifle aimed towards the jungle, Tex DeAugustine stepped down and stood near the vehicle, while other wreckers were rumbling towards the ambush site, churning up dust.

Within the chaos, a commander's orders could be heard, concise and decisive, but with compassion for the task of his men.

DeAugustine and the driver from E Company had been sent to the coordinates to tow back the damaged dump trucks. The commander and his group of soldiers were there to haul away the bodies.

In an early morning ambush, the Vietcong had been waiting, hidden within the jungle, and when the convoy had reached the target area, the VC had fired on full automatic from both sides of the road. The cross fire struck in horizontal arcs across the transit trucks, leaving a spray of bullet holes in the tin that now lured spears of light.

Vehicles slanted precariously, rammed down against the slope of the road. The soldiers who had not had time to escape the trucks were slumped over in their seats against the steering wheels or leaning heavily against the battered doors.

With DeAugustine keeping watch, the driver swung around, aligned the wrecker and backed about three feet from the front of a vacant dump truck. Getting out of the cab, he then stepped up on a tire, pulling himself into the operator's seat, and lowered the boom, the hook swinging on the blackened steel cable.

Some of the ambushed soldiers had leapt from the dump trucks for cover, while trying to defend themselves against a hidden enemy. These dead soldiers lay on the road and in the ditches, dirt and blood darkening their uniforms, rifles dropped just beyond their fingers.

Loneliness lingered over the place like a cold fog. . .a loneliness of soldiers who had been far away from home and realized that their lives had come to such an end, having been shot and simply wanting someone with them while they died.

With dump trucks offering insufficient fire power and protection against the attack, those soldiers who had kept alive longer, who had watched as their ammunition ran low and their number became less and less, had merely prolonged their despair and desperation.

When the Vietcong eventually emerged from the jungle, the injured understood that they would fare no better than their dead Brothers.

These injured soldiers had closed their eyes, each trying to find one last thought to dull the knowledge of the inevitable approaching of death, bracing for the shadow to hover, and the barrel of an AK-47 to drift over into direct aim and then the click before the crack, before the end.

DeAugustine positioned the bar and waited for the hook, hearing the driver's voice and following his directions. The scene around him played like a slow, blurry tragedy, soldiers having been given grievous parts without choice. In the distance, three jets streaked over, napalm silver canisters tumbling through blue sky.

The other soldiers worked quietly, urgently, methodically, tugging the dead from the trucks, sometimes stepping up to lean in and loosen a soldier's boots from the pedals before allowing the weight of the body to fall into their arms. They briefly looked into the faces, following streams of red from under the helmets and then shifted their glance and grip for hauling.

Getting down on his knee, a soldier turned a body over, the arm flopping against the ground. The pale face rolled sideways and then rested on a slight tilt, the dead boy's stare oblivious to the bright sun. Two soldiers leaned over, one grabbing the wrists and the other clutching around the ankles of the boots, and shuffled towards an operational dump truck. With an understood timing, they swung the soldier upward onto the back of the truck, the body thumping against the metal.

A procession of soldiers followed, heaving the weight of the dead, the bodies rolling forward, knocking against the others, Brother against Brother. . .a final journey home.

As he secured the hook, DeAugustine heard the slightly strained rhythm of the soldiers walking past. His consciousness shuddered, trying to leap over reality, but instead falling into bleak nothingness. On that day he vowed that he would not end up like those boys.

Again and again, the other soldiers hoisted the dead from the ditches, down from the convoy trucks and up onto the back of the operational dump truck, their hands sticky red.

Loose rifles were gathered and thrown alongside of the bodies, clanking against the helmets and creating a crisscrossed heap.

The wrecker driver eased the lever, and the winch creaked while pulleys screeched against the weight of the rising dump truck. When the cable was locked in place, DeAugustine got into the wrecker, and he and the driver began back towards base, the scene slowly fading by a curtain of dust.

Time in Nam resounded with the cracks of AK-47s, the roar of mortars, the boom of tossed grenades, the hiss of rockets and the echo of detonated mines. This thundering of war could be understood and accepted. The quiet of soldiers who walked amongst their fallen Brothers could perhaps be explained. In the end, it was neither the thunder of war that soldiers most feared, nor even the quiet soldiers kept. What soldiers could not forget was the sound of death, the emptiness of the end. . .the only silence of war.

.45 Auto

He would take a grenade, keeping his fingers pressed against the release lever, yank out the cotter pin and slip the pin back into place. . .seven or eight times. He knew my attention never strayed from that loose grenade in his hand, and he heard plenty of cussing from me every time he amused himself with my agitation.

I had been away from base for awhile, and when I returned, he walked over, standing about two feet in front of me, and began a conversation while unhooking a grenade from his belt. He kept talking, but I stopped listening, because he had that grenade against his palm, with his fingers working the cotter pin free. Mid-sentence, he gasped and glanced up with a look of dread as the grenade tumbled from his hand.

I ran towards the bunker, counting down the seven seconds, my boots slipping on the gravel, until I was scrambling forward on all fours and had about a second and a half to spare when I cleared the corner. Flat on the ground, my arms over my head, I waited for the explosion.

Nothing happened.

With my knees and wrists scraped from the escape, I crawled from the dirt. He was laughing. He had detonated the blasting cap earlier. Entertainment. . . I guess.

He and I routinely bought off beer rations from the guys

in camp who didn't drink. We had a refrigerator with a tow chain wrapped around and secured with a padlock, in which fit two and a half cases. We shared our fortune with the other tankers, but we didn't want anyone stealing our beer while we were gone.

One evening, when I was working on an engine at the Tank Park, a lieutenant and his driver pulled up in a jeep, and we drove back to the barracks.

Apparently, while I had been away on my latest mission, my friend's bunk mates had noticed him physically declining. By the time they realized that he had malaria, their decision to advance upon him as a group only intensified the paranoia brought on by his high fever.

When I reached the barracks, a few guys were standing by the entrance, glancing inside but keeping shielded from possible gunfire.

Sitting in the corner between the bunks and a row of lockers, he had his back against the wall, his knees drawn up, and his boot heels braced against the floor. His finger was on the trigger of his .45. Sweat dripped from his hair, down his neck, darkening his shirt and giving his pale face a lifeless appearance.

Cautiously I walked over and sat on the far end of a bunk, diagonally across from him. He kept the gun aimed in my direction, his elbows tight against his ribs in an effort to stop the shaking of his hands. His eyes were wide with a frenzied, ferocious panic like a German shepherd backed against an electric fence.

He kept repeating that everyone was plotting to get him, and I kept trying to convince him otherwise. His eyes narrowed, and he leaned forward, tightening his grip on the gun. With a glance towards the floor in front of his feet, he vowed that he would shoot anyone who crossed his line.

I promised him that I would protect him. He stared blankly and insisted that they were all against him. I assured him that I would not let that happen. Then I asked if he would give me the .45 that was aimed in my direction, knocking against the inside of his trembling knees.

He wiped his brow with the back of his wrist, scrutinizing me in an effort to trust his friend, gave a weary sigh and handed over the gun.

With the .45 stuck through my belt, the other soldiers ventured into the barracks. He snatched up his bayonet and held the long, slender blade in front of him. I stepped between him and the other soldiers. They looked at the knife, at me and slowly exited.

Again I sat down, but now nearer, across from him. I told him that I would keep him safe. He listened, rocking back and forth with the blade tilting in his hand. Eventually he leaned against the wall, his shoulders slumping and gave me the knife.

I pulled him up, and we walked over by the door where the guys had already secured a straight jacket. He turned towards me. I nodded.

Keeping their eyes averted from his face, one of his bunk mates slipped on the sleeves and then fastened the clasps, while another soldier crossed his arms over his stomach and tugged the sleeves around his waist, where they tied the strings in the back. He stood quietly, with a confused, weary expression.

In the jeep, he sat between me and another soldier from his barracks. When we reached the Medic building, he whispered that he did not want to go, but I assured him that he would be OK.

The doctor walked out to the jeep and gently explained that everything was going to be alright as he sunk in the syringe needle.

That would be the last time I saw him, being led away, strapped in the straight jacket, his unruly blond hair wet from the fever, his eyes half closed, staring at nothing, and a lost look on his dusty face.

A new kid took over his bunk, his tank crew found another loader, and other soldiers drank the cold beer.

I kept his .45.

THE ROCK PILE

What did those soldiers think about while they waited under the sweltering sun? What did those soldiers think about while they watched for the enemy? What did those soldiers think about while guarding a ridge of rock? What did those soldiers think about while they waited with their weapons on a rock pile, knowing that they were going to die?

Orders came down that I was to be transported to a place north of Kontum to fix a bridge tank that had broken down in enemy territory. I gathered my tool box, M-16, ammo, flak jacket, a couple bandoliers, my gas mask and three atropine syrettes. The atropine was an antidote against nerve gas…didn't always work. We never went anywhere without our gas masks.

With the sun beating down, easily 100 degrees in the shade, I walked the third of a mile with the 90 pound tool box and ended up being late, the UH-1 chopper already waiting.

The jungle spun past below, hot air gusting through the doors and the chopper's blades thwacking. Besides the pilot, co-pilot, and the door gunner, there were nine other infantry soldiers. A few of these soldiers had just been brought over…wearing nice clean uniforms. They sat in the center, keeping their eyes averted. The guys who had already been in country for awhile had taken the outside spots, dangling their legs over the edge, their boots above the runners. A couple of soldiers sat on their banged up helmets, in case we got shot at from below.

These infantry soldiers were being transported to *The Rock Pile*. This place, being of higher altitude within the mountain range of the Central Highlands, was considered a strategic location. The vantage point enabled our troops to observe the area below.

If the Vietcong secured The Rock Pile, they could observe our military activities for miles and gain knowledge of our helicopters, fighter jets, tanks and vehicles. If the Vietcong secured this vantage point, they would discover the location of our troops and then organize ambushes.

Strategically, the U.S. military believed essential that The Rock Pile be kept at all cost.

From above, the place looked vast and gray. As the chopper approached nearer, we could make out the rocks and boulders, a few towering over 20 feet high. . .nothing pretty, just grim, gray, jagged rock. No place to dig a fox hole. No place to take cover. The pilot circled around the area. The door gunner peered down below, slowly swinging his M-60.

The nine soldiers waited with stoic expressions, while clutching their M-16s. They had heard about The Rock Pile.

The experienced soldiers accepted their fate. . .fear got put into a different place. The new boys were terrified.

The pilot steadied the chopper, hovered above the ground, but did not land. The nine soldiers, burdened down by their rucksacks, ammo and weapons, jumped down, thumping on the barren pile of rock to join the other two platoons. Once unloaded, they quickly got into their defensive positions.

The pilot gave an honoring salute before lifting off in a fury of dust, trying to promptly exit from the place where he had just transported a group of guys.

I glanced down. No place to dig a fox hole. No place to take cover.

As we leveled off, I asked the pilot about The Rock Pile. He told me how they had been supplying the place with ammunition, weapons, medical supplies, C rations, water and soldiers for a long time.

When the pilot got busy with tricky chopper maneuvers, trying to avoid being shot, the co-pilot continued the story, while the door gunner fired at the muzzle flashes from the valley below.

According to the pilots, group after group of grunts had been unloaded to fend off the enemy on that ridge of rock. The Vietcong, knowing the strategic significance of the location, would overtake the place using rockets, mortars and eventually a direct assault. Another American troop would then be given the task to take back The Rock Pile and try keeping the location defended.

As far as these two pilots knew, the longest any group of soldiers had been at The Rock Pile before being overrun, and every last soldier killed, was seven and a half weeks. . .seven and a half weeks. The group of soldiers left behind on that desolate place was promised nothing better than seven and a half weeks, but then The Rock Pile had to be kept at all cost.

BEYOND THE PERIMETER

The blades' rhythm reverberated through the air, as Vietcong scattered below, flashes bursting from their AK-47s. The door gunner braced himself against the M-60, his back and shoulders jolting with the force of the bandolier snapping through the machine gun, the brass shells clinking, rolling over the sand bags and sprinkling over the edge. I was kneeling by the door, rifle aimed down, deafened by the engine drone, while gusts of air created a hollow echo.

The gunner slowly swiveled the M-60, checked the chopper for damage and then leaned against the door frame. We had earlier dropped off nine infantry soldiers at *The Rock Pile* and were flying north, our runners nearly skimming the trees. Over another ridge, we again encountered enemy fire, but the gunner merely stood behind the M-60, having already considered the distance and the enemy's faulty aim.

We landed two and a half miles west of a temporary base. I grabbed my toolbox and jumped out. A broken down bridge tank waited for me, along with the two-man crew.

After quickly concluding that the fuel injector pump was shot, we took a jeep to the nearby base, which consisted of a central command bunker, infantry dug in, with timbers placed across a few of the fox holes, and only meager concertina wire separating the troops from the surrounding jungle.

The 1st and 69th Armor Divisions were there, along with approximately 25 gun tanks, dulled by the dust of red dirt and positioned in a circle around the perimeter. The mechanics, tired of trying to do their job while being shot at by snipers, worked within that circle of tanks. Rumor had it that $50.00 and time off were the rewards that the Vietcong earned for each U.S. mechanic killed.

I ordered a new injector pump, talked with a few of the guys whom I had known at diesel school, and then drove back, one of the tankers following in his VTR.

He aligned the VTR with the bridge tank, raised the boom while watching me for hand signals, until I could connect the cable to the bridge. He swung the bridge over and onto the ground and then repositioned at the rear of the bridge tank, where we removed the rear deck plating from off the top of the engine.

As the sky darkened with a fiery horizon, eight soldiers from the Cavalry arrived. One of their personnel carriers had a hole behind the driver's hatch from a B-40 rocket. The crew told me how they had seen the rocket streaking towards them and had escaped through the hatches before the rocket exploded.

I crawled inside to check out the damage. The torn metal indicated that the rocket had hit between where the men would have been sitting.

That evening, we sat around the armored vehicles drinking beer and recounting our adventures, without the restraint of rank, for the commanding officers had removed their epaulets so as not to be targeted.

These soldiers talked with each other like brothers. . . boys who had together battled against the enemy and also the intangible perils of fear and doubt and despair that could as easily unravel a group of soldiers. They told their stories with the unspoken truth that their lives would always be connected as would be their deaths. At times they became briefly quiet, their expressions revealing a part of the story that could not be told in words.

These eight soldiers knew that I understood the emotion of their camaraderie. They knew that I had seen their stories within the darkness of my own time in Nam.

Later that night, two soldiers from the bridge tank and I took turns on guard duty. The light slowly faded into a black ink over the jungle. We had no heavy weapons, limited men and our tank had no motor. With my .45, I sat between the cross bars of the bridge on the tank, squinting into a complete darkness where I could not see beyond the gleam of the metal. Every creak of the cooling iron became the Vietcong crawling up behind me.

With the morning light, the Cavalry pulled out for a search and destroy mission, joining the infantry. The extra grunts rode on top of the personnel carriers, garbed for battle, their legs over the edge.

Yet waiting on the replacement injector pump, I decided to investigate a small, square hut that stood beyond the perimeter, near the jungle. The building appeared built of concrete, with a grass roof, a large empty window on one side and a door with a small window on the other side, an unusual, isolated building that held no apparent purpose. I began that direction, but when I had reached half way, I felt a cold shiver, like a presence descending as a warning or threat. I halted, locked on that invisible line, trying to listen without looking like I was listening. Then I slowly turned and began walking away, wondering when the bullet would take me down. I kept my stride calm, but I could feel my heart racing. I knew that the Vietcong were watching. They were always watching our soldiers, tracking our movements and studying our strategies. I had ventured beyond the perimeter, a place not invited, crossing a line that would not be tolerated.

Early that afternoon, only two soldiers from the Cavalry returned. Beyond the perimeter, they had watched soldiers die, including four of their own crew. The returning soldiers spoke of the tactical maneuvers, the combined operation, the ferocity of the battle, but they did not talk about their dead.

The power that death had to change soldiers could always be felt. Every soldier experienced his share of death, but even within the inevitable constant casualties of war there existed times of truly personal loss.

As the two soldiers got into the back of another APC to retrieve the last three personnel carriers, the emptiness became like the tolling of a bell, an echoing despair that crushes that flicker of hope so desperately sought in war.

That emptiness followed me, and I wanted to forget the suffering, the hopelessness, the faces of the four Cavalry soldiers with whom I had talked with the night before…the four soldiers who had died, but I knew that their deaths would forever be connected with my life.

That night, I walked the quarter of a mile to a friendly Vietnamese village. While exploring the village, a family invited me into their dwelling. Despite the little that they owned, they offered me a place at their table. The men talked of the land and of the past, while the women offered gracious hospitality and the children scurried amongst the chickens. They were all eager to give of their friendship in return for the courtesy I extended to their family and the customs of their village.

The injector pump arrived the next day. I aligned the timing gears and began hooking up the lines. When it got too dark to work, I walked back to the village.

That night the Vietcong pursued with an aggressive attack. The village men grabbed their rifles and positioned themselves for defense. In that I would not be allowed to join the defense, the women and children led me into a hidden building, about 10 by 12 with only a four foot high ceiling. I kept my hand on my .45, watching the armed ARVAN near me, while listening as the VC walked mortars across the village, creating a thundering vibration of splintering wood, followed by the drumming rain of pieces falling.

When I returned the next morning, the sergeant approached, his face flushed, the muscles in his jaw quivering, his lips pressed tight together, until I was standing in front of him, and then his wrath exploded. He asked me what the hell I was thinking, because he sure wasn't going to get blamed for my being captured, and I better not go back or I would be damn sorry.

I stood there, my hands in my pockets, keeping my attention protocol compliant. . .not really listening. I figured that he was glad to see me.

With the sun brimming the sky, a convoy arrived, including my commander and another soldier in the VTR, with the expectation that once I completed my task, I would return with them to Camp Enari. That did not happen. While finishing the repairs on the bridge tank, a radio call from headquarters gave orders for my transfer.

With the altering of agenda, my commander and four other soldiers decided to stay the night in that isolated area beyond the base, and despite the dangers of dusk, two

Vietnamese women from the village walked the quarter of a mile to warn those soldiers that the VC were planning to kill them that night. Only for the bravery and risk of those women leaving their village at that hour were the lives of five soldiers spared.

What *had* happened, following my repair of the bridge tank, was that when the chopper arrived, I grabbed my 90 pound tool box and crawled in. The chopper lifted and increased speed, the gusts of air creating a hollow echo.

A broken down gun tank waited for me, along with the four-man crew.

POINT MAN

I fell forward onto my knees, and then onto my stomach, my elbows striking the ground, rifle ready. Our group had been fanned across the ridge, moving forward. The other platoon had been maneuvering down a steep slope, one behind the next, using the muzzle of their rifles to separate the elephant grass, when their Point Man fired his M-16 on full auto.

Half of our group scrambled behind the few trees, while the other seven of us soldiers hit the ground.

I tipped my helmet back and slowly pulled myself into the lowest area within reach, a two inch deep indentation in the dirt...better coverage than nothing. The steam of wet, swampy soil filled my lungs, while water soaked through my boots and pants as I tried to press myself lower.

The Vietcong force would be more than our combined platoons. They would surround us, and we had no tank, no heavy artillery and no realistic escape.

The guys near me glanced over, their jaws clamped tight, hoping to keep their breathing quiet and their position motionless, as if we could take cover behind nothing and yet not be noticed.

The last twang of the Point Man's M-16 echoed in the air, and the sergeant signaled to his radio man. Trying to keep down low, the RTO unclipped the microphone from his shirt and handed it over, the spiraled cord stretching across his shoulder. The sergeant waited a moment as if listening and then asked for a situation report.

Every soldier near enough shifted slightly in order to hear. The rest of the guys tried to read our expressions. The sergeant held down the button a second time and again asked for an explanation. No reply came back.

Returning the speaker to his RTO, the sergeant took a deep breath and motioned for us to advance forward.

Advance forward into an ambush? We hesitated. We had no tank or heavy artillery.

Fear, like a hot current, surged through me, a painful panic, numbing my thinking and strangling my breath. Death waited for soldiers, the eventuality of it all, not in the end to be denied the recompense of war, and on that day, I could feel death aiming an AK-47 at my chest. My muscles froze in that shallow incline of dirt, and I struggled against the instinct to keep down and hold onto life, even if life had become little better than watching death.

The sergeant continued forward, his RTO alongside of him, the radio antenna swaying. Some soldiers traded off the advantage of the few trees for a second of coverage.

Unsteadily I began crawling, using the instep of my boots to force myself forward, scuffing my elbows and knees across the ground, while praying to every God of every religion I could remember, gods of the past ages, and even a few mythical gods, in the chance that one Almighty Power would consider sparing us on that day.

Nearer the edge of the ridge, I got onto my feet, but crouched over, the butt of my rifle tight against my ribs, and my finger on the trigger.

The platoon of soldiers below were gathered together, their gestures erratic, their voices escalating in nervous commotion.

The sergeant radioed down.

A reply came back. . .*big snake*.

The RTO frowned. The sergeant asked for an *affirmative* on what he thought he had heard, and then we saw the rigid 13 foot high elephant grass sway violently and bow back, in a stretch of nearly 20 feet, as the length, strength and weight of the snake cut through the terrain.

We watched and waited until the grass stopped swaying, and then our group hastened down the slope.

Gripping his M-16, the Point Man described the snake as being nearly 300 pounds, and the yellow brown bulk of the body, with black crossing camouflaging rings, easily large enough to swallow him. The soldiers from his platoon nodded in agreement.

According to the Point Man, when he had stepped through the wall of grass, the orange glassy eyes had locked on him, and the snake lunged, seemingly lofting over the terrain, its narrowing, heavy head swaying towards the soldiers, its jaw wide open, exhaling deep hisses while spiked teeth reached for its prey.

The platoon had run backwards, sloshing through the swamp, their boots being snared by soggy roots. The Point Man had fired on full auto, and emptied nearly two clips before the snake decided that the soldier wasn't worth the risk.

Wiping his hand across the back of his neck, the Point Man looked out over the swamp, knowing that we yet needed to walk the rest of the way across. I looked out over the swamp, my fear evaporated, knowing that we had only engaged a big snake.

For Those Who Saved Our Soldiers

Daniel Michael Pruitt scrambled off the military cot, reaching for his M-16 rifle that he had positioned on the hooks inside the door of his five ton bridge truck.

His weapon was gone.

A cobalt blue sky in the chasm hour of night had dimmed the barracks and bunkers of LZ St. George, but had not shadowed enough the Vietcong exiting the tattered, exploded side of one of the company tents less than ten feet away. The enemy was approaching with swift, edgy strides, an expression of tension and the trained action of his finger on the trigger, his AK-47 leveled on Pruitt.

He fired.

The bullet struck Pruitt in the left thigh, shattering over two inches of his femur, slicing through an artery, yanking him a quarter turn off balance, before collapsing him forward, flat onto the ground.

Pruitt struggled onto his knees, then unsteadily to his feet, attempting to reach the only obtainable coverage, a bucket tractor behind piled sand bags nearly 25 feet away. His leg immediately buckled, and he fell back onto the ground, a second bullet ripping through his right knee.

Within the muzzle flashes sparking the darkness, and bullets shrilling past him, heightening the shift of energy already resonating through camp, Pruitt hastily considered his options.

He tried again, attempting to drag himself forward, but the steady gush of blood seeping through his pants was claiming the last of his strength. He was now caught in a cross fire, cornered, wounded, without a weapon.

Sprawled on his stomach, his left arm shielding his head, and the VC yet approaching, Pruitt closed his eyes, breathing in the dirt of the earth, knowing that he needed to lie still, because that remained his only option.

A third bullet struck him in the left calf, fracturing bone, his muscles jerking, striking his boot against his numbing right leg. He heard the continued crack of bullets around him, as if the VC was now standing close range, shooting down at him on auto fire. He knew that he needed to keep quiet against the panic, and stifled his breathing, jaw clamped closed, the desperation for air pressing against his chest.

The fourth bullet cut into his right hip, though Pruitt, now fading within a disorienting weakness, barely noticed as blood continued to soak his uniform with a nauseating warmth. A fifth bullet snapped the bone of his left arm, jolting his hand, but his instinctive defense had already expected and ignored the pain.

The focus of Pruitt's consciousness became the accuracy of a final shot that would take what was left of him. Engulfed in darkness, his vision obscured against the red dirt, he expected that final shot, and the waiting became like a slow falling…an emotional flailing down an empty abyss without control, except for that one critical survival thought, again and again, to keep quiet. . .play dead, while bracing for that instant of explosive mortal shattering before the end. Trapped in this solitary nightmare, Pruitt believed that at the age of 20, he was going to die.

Cross fire continued, the VC crept forward, Pruitt keeping quiet...playing dead as the VC then leaned his weight on Pruitt's shoulder and climbed over him, escaping towards the bridge truck and crawled onto the axle.

Pruitt was an E Company 4th Engineer of Camp Enari, but he had been sent as part of a convoy to LZ St. George to deliver ammunition...crucial ammunition that would now give the soldiers of the LZ a far better defense against the infiltrated enemy. Pruitt had been the last to unload his truck, and by that time, the shadows of dusk prowled the land, keeping him at St. George for the night.

Despite the disorienting impact of his injuries, he understood the situation. With only two months left of his tour, he lay dying in a pool of red, while other soldiers endured each their own dire fate in the darkness of a terrible attack. Pruitt called for a medic, hoping that he could yet be helped.

Keeping low, the medic hurried over, squatted beside Pruitt and rolled him onto his back, the broken bones causing his arm and leg to loll in an awkward angle. Pruitt promptly alerted the medic to the concealed location of the VC, and the soldier nodded, yet focusing his attention on his work, trying to stifle the worst of the bleeding, while talking to Pruitt in a calm and comforting tone.

Pruitt's breathing slowed, an unfamiliar fatigue dragging him further and further away. Knowing that he now had this soldier beside him gratefully eased enough of his concern, because even with effort, he knew that he could no longer keep conscious. He heard the medic talking to him, but the words began sounding like slurred echoes drifting in a dimming haze, until only quiet and blackness existed.

Having been hauled to the medical tent of LZ St. George,

Pruitt felt the cold of the table, and heard the crashing of mortars and tracer rounds that continued erupting like distant static, mingled with the drone of arriving gun ships. Chaotic urgency surrounded him, doctors trying to stabilize other arriving injured soldiers within the bursts of light. He vaguely realized that he was part of that urgency, as a doctor leaned over him, tugging at his bloodied uniform to contend with the five gun shot wounds, Pruitt being lost in a daze, not reacting, his limbs feeling heavy and numb, and images of reality shuffling around him like an incoherent dream.

With a distracted confusion, he barely comprehended the thwacking of blades, the slight jarring of his injuries as two soldiers hoisted his stretcher onto the chopper, and then the gust of warm air and tilting momentum as the chopper lifted off.

Pruitt awoke without a weapon, trapped, unable to defend himself, the clamor of voices and circumstances that he did not recognize. He lunged forward, ripping out the IV tube that had been taped against his wrist, trying to break loose of the contraptions, the confines of casts and metal rods and cables of traction, before two doctors came rushing over to his bed, holding him back, offering a reassuring explanation that for Pruitt, became little better than a faulty rationale in his delirious, frantic effort to escape.

The severity of his injuries, the fever and detriments of discovered malaria and the intravenous morphine kept Pruitt teetering between consciousness, unconsciousness and that elusive realm that lingers beyond. At times, when he closed his eyes, Pruitt believed that the end of his bed was rising, and he would hastily secure his perimeter to avoid being toppled. During hours of restless sleep, images of the war flashed in scattered scenes and confusing outcomes, prompting Pruitt to maintain a delusional vigilance. Within his delusional vigilance, Pruitt thought that the VC, who had shot him at St. George, now lurked and stalked by the hospital windows, waiting to fire that final shot.

Balanced on that precarious edge between life and death, Pruitt also experienced a vision where he drifted through a prism of light, the rainbow colors leading him away. During that experience, he understood that he was dying, allowing his life to end.

While contending with the complications of his injuries, Pruitt noted one day, a ranking officer with two other soldiers approaching his direction. One of the soldiers glanced at the chart, and then the ranking officer stated Pruitt's name for verification. Pruitt nodded, trying to comprehend the purpose of the unusual official visit.

With the two soldiers standing like sentinels, guarding with respect the significance of the tribute, the ranking officer, with a chivalrous demeanor, presented a box and lifted the cover, revealing a Purple Heart medal.

The ranking officer spoke with sincerity and high regard, but with Pruitt's emotions nearly breaking, he could not focus on the words.

He felt proud to have received such an honor, but beyond the gratitude, he felt embraced by an enduring camaraderie with those soldiers within the 71st Evac, while emotionally acknowledging all the soldiers who had died. During difficult days of recovery, the Purple Heart yet reflected every other recovering soldier's continued courage.

When Pruitt could keep awake, he talked with the other soldiers in near proximity and observed the professional efficiency of the 71st Evac. Doctors roamed the aisles with a determined pace, reviewing medical charts, talking with the injured soldiers, answering the difficult questions and offering honest encouragement.

The nurses circled through the rows of wounded men with quiet competence, pleasant smiles and cheerful conversations, giving help whenever needed...whatever the task required.

Despite the doctors and nurses' own weariness and their own battered emotions from watching, day after day, soldiers suffering and dying, they pursued their duties with intensity, compassion and sacrifice.

Pruitt had experienced during his time in Nam the truths of war, but within the 71st Evac, he watched an emotional truth...soldiers struggling against pain and loss and images that would never be forgotten. The nurses and doctors worked within that pain, within that loss and gathered their own enduring images.

Daniel Michael Pruitt would be returning home to his family, a fortunate fate that he knew had been nearly taken, and he felt an overwhelming gratitude towards the LZ St. George medics and doctors, the medics of the dustoff chopper and the doctors and nurses of the 71st Evac...quiet heroes of war, those men and women who endured war's emotional reality and kept watch on that edge between life and death in order to save our soldiers.

Craig Johnson halted the jeep near the entrance door, and with the satchel of Pruitt's mail, followed the lieutenant. The sun scorched down, casting a hazy glimmer across the pale blue sky which loomed like a fading tarp behind the expanse of strategically scattered medical buildings.

Johnson kept his stride in pace with the lieutenant's agenda, but his thoughts faltered with wariness. He knew how expertly the weapons of war could slash through the lives of soldiers, abandoning those boys within the struggle of irreparable injuries and exhausting recoveries. He braced himself for that truth. . .the inevitable reality waiting for him within the 71st Evac.

Johnson and the lieutenant stepped inside, the light of the sun suddenly dimmed, replaced by the stringent scene of rows of bandaged soldiers.

Time within the fury of battle tends to flicker past in confusing pictures that abruptly get yanked away by the quick colliding of fear and adrenaline, training and instinct, camaraderie and heroism, but time within the 71st Evac seemed to slow with an urgent grip, like the mysterious flow of a dream, blurred with vivid images, echoing in details and poignancy even after the dream has ended.

Despite the calm conversations humming through the place, there existed a somber quiet, as if the unspoken thoughts of the soldiers lingered like trapped emotional energy within that quiet. . .intense emotions of anger and uncertainty, gratitude and despair, courage and pain, creating a pendulum of reality which held both the bleak loneliness that followed the panic and agony of soldiers confronting the complications of their injuries and a protective reverence that honored those who had died and those trying to survive.

Johnson walked between the hospital beds, a few soldiers glancing up at him, their stoic expressions keeping hidden the grief of their stories. Johnson didn't need to hear their stories to understand what they had endured, and although he knew that so much wanted to be spoken for these men. . .words of respect, encouragement or comfort, nothing could be said to change the tragic consequences of war.

What words could he properly offer to boys who had nearly died, now shackled by their injuries, while the deaths of their Brothers crossed freely through their thoughts?

Having thus far been spared, Johnson became one of the fortunate, and all he could give back to these Brothers was his unwavering loyalty.

The pictures resounding within that place brought upon Johnson an engulfing sadness. He wanted to be wrong. He wanted the images to be an imagined illusion, but he was walking within the truth. . .doctors overwhelmed by the vastness of their responsibilities, nurses too young for such trials, and a room of soldiers torn by bullets, sliced by shrapnel, ripped by explosions. . .boys who should have been accomplishing the blessings of life. . .not carrying the crosses of war.

The 71st Evac, like a foretelling mirror of the past and present, reflected the future of the war, and within that reflection, Johnson knew that he could, with one wrong step of fate, eventually become part of that image. The truth would not end with his exit from the hospital.

Soldiers would arrive day after day, and within those days yet to happen, soldiers would die. Other soldiers would survive and find themselves on a precarious edge that neither claimed their mortality nor gave them back the entirety of their lives.

With slow strides, Johnson acknowledged each soldier's suffering, while not wanting to get lost in the pain of the place. . .the anguish in the faces, the vacant expressions, sleep fraught with flashbacks, boys with missing limbs. Despite his effort to keep resilient, he felt himself so easily ushered into the despair.

The reasons for war are rarely accurately explained, but the end is always the same.

Craig Johnson would be returning to Camp Enari, and eventually, hopefully going home, leaving the 71st Evac far away in the distance, but he already knew that the images could neither be forgotten nor left far away. The images of the 71st Evac allotted no distance, only the stark truth of sacrifice.

THE PROMISE

I didn't know his name or rank or how long he had yet in Vietnam. His platoon was geared up for a mission off base, but I didn't know where. None of that really mattered.

He had black hair, brown eyes and a slight build that made him appear younger than the soldiers who sat alongside of him.

The three-quarter ton vehicle stopped next to us, and he was in the back, an M-16 held tight against his shoulder.

He was trembling, his breathing rapid and uneven, and his voice cracked with an effort not to cry while he spoke. *Promise me if I don't come back, you won't forget me. Promise me if I don't come back, you won't forget me.*

The other soldiers tipped their helmets lower and looked away or down on their boots.

With his fingers curled into fists, he pleaded again. *Promise me if I don't come back, you won't forget me!*

Understanding his desperation, I looked at him and promised that I would not forget him. I said those words because he needed to hear them, so that he would have the courage to go on and do what he had to do, even if that meant dying.

As the three-quarter ton vehicle pulled away, he leaned back and stared at me, as if to remember the soldier with whom he had trusted his mortality and immortality.

He did not come back.

This is all I know of his story, but the little I know is all I have left for to honor him.

Soldier, I have kept my promise. I have not forgotten you.

Until later Brother
200a out

ELEVEN BRAVO

They wrote last letters home. . .soldiers sitting on the edge of their bunks or in foxholes, the paper pressed against their drawn up knees as they tried to envision themselves dead.

They imagined how their mothers would cry, and how their fathers would read the letter and walk away, lost in a silence of pride and agony.

They imagined their friends standing together, talking about what kind of guy they had been, even though they knew that they had changed with the war.

The soldiers wrote letters home, trying to describe the depth of their fears and anguish, without writing about the images that haunted them most. . .the watching of death and bodies being hauled away. They wanted to write about these horrendous things, because they did not know where else to put the pain, but they could not explain accurately or emotionally enough how the relentless loss of fellow soldiers had taken a toll on the essence of their existence.

These soldiers wrote their last will and testaments, sorting through in their thoughts who they wanted given the few precious things they had once owned. . .their dog or car or hunting rifle. . .significant decisions for boys.

They wrote last letters home, because their illusions of combat immortality quickly faded when they had seen other equally daring soldiers get killed.

Each soldier wrote down what needed to be known, while hoping that his family would never have to read his last letter.

A hill within the Central Highlands proved to be a location where the elevation gave the enemy the advantage of firing upon U.S. troops.

For our infantry, in an effort to secure the crucial area, the location required an arduous climb through treacherous jungle terrain where the Vietcong tethered poisonous snakes, contrived booby traps and grenades that used slender vines as tripwires, camouflaged with a covering of leaves vertically lined sharpened bamboo rods called punji sticks and buried bouncing betties. . .explosives that with one wrong step propelled upward before detonating with a showering down of shrapnel in a wide umbrella arc over an entire platoon.

Prior to our infantry's effort, Artillery Hill launched explosive rounds that ripped up the land, the impact resonating under the boots of our waiting soldiers.

Then the jets flew over, usually three in V formation, streaking across the sky, dropping bombs on the hill top with strategic accuracy.

Our infantry watched. . .waited, the haze of dirt drifting from the height of the hill, as the napalm burned through the foliage, leaving wisps of white snaking down the green slope.

The couple hundred infantry then maneuvered their way through the jungle that rose at a 45 degree angle, and at times nearly vertical. Toppled trees hindered their pace, tangled vines ensnared their boots, the heat of a sultry sun challenged their perseverance and the traps of the enemy relentlessly dared their vigilance.

One soldier behind the next, these boys used the vines like ropes to pull themselves forward, as the point man hacked through with his bayonet. They endeavored upward, giving a slight shove to the soldier in front when his boots began slipping.

When the infantry neared the top of the hill, the VC attacked with grenades, AK-47s and machine guns.

Those infantry soldiers who reached the summit then contended with close range combat, insufficient cover and an outnumbering enemy.

Medics hastened within the battle, trying to ease injured soldiers' panic while they administered morphine, applied compress bandages and tied tourniquets.

Chosen soldiers then promptly began back with the injured. The wounded that could walk, stumbled through the jungle, leaning heavily on the other soldiers.

For the men who could not walk, soldiers hoisted them over their shoulders and trudged forward, while trying to shift the limp weight as they steadied their balance on the slope, focusing their endurance on helping their Brothers survive.

Week after week, the infantry pursued the summit in shifts of platoons. At the end of each day, they retrieved the bodies of their men. Grinding their heels into the slanting earth, the strongest soldiers gripped the boots of the dead and dragged the bodies, blood smearing over the leaves as they slowly descended down.

These soldiers did not only carry the weight of their Brothers, they carried the weight of death, the crushing grief that emotionally exhausts a soldier when he has watched his friends die day after day, and must grip the boots of a man who had earlier stood beside him and drag that soldier from the jungle.

The men following watched the bodies being yanked over the wet terrain, ashen faces altered by death, arms extended above their heads, with rigid fingers flopping against the ground.

Dustoff choppers waited at the base of the hill, the wounded and the dead being hauled away together. The remaining soldiers sat alone in their foxholes, trying to forget, because they would tomorrow climb. . .battle. . .die.

There exists no true victory in war, no worthy recompense in walking away from a battle while other soldiers died.

Last letters were found in the task of emptying lost soldiers' lockers. Last letters were found on the bodies hauled back from battles, the folded papers having been slid carefully by the boys within a strap of their helmets.

Mothers cried.

Fathers walked away in silence.

VC Valley

Below the ridge of the LZ and beyond the steep slopes, a towering jungle kept hidden thousands of Vietcong. During the darkness, they would crawl from the green fortress and turn our claymore mines around. If a soldier then pressed the clacker trigger, a 60 degree arc of approximately 700 steel shrapnel fragments would fire 100 meters back into the landing zone.

VC Valley challenged a soldier's courage, and for any soldier unfortunate enough to be destined the assignment, the location increased his probability of death. This place, VC Valley, was where we were going next.

The convoy included a couple gun tanks, trucks carrying troops, and our VTR, the *War Wagon*, kicking up a cloud of dust that made it difficult for the enemy to target the last in line. I drove, with Gibbs behind the .50 caliber machine gun and a young buck sergeant, David Conrad, in the passenger hatch.

The convoy traveled for about four hours, before halting near a Montagnard village. Conrad insisted that I take a break, so Gibbs took over the driving. Conrad got behind the .50 caliber, and I crawled up on top of the tank.

The convoy began rolling forward through the village, with the Montagnards standing on both sides of the path.

The tribal men, wearing simple loin cloths, observed our approach while leaning on their spears, and the boys watched with bows slung over their shoulders.

The women wore drab colored wraps with bright fringes around their waists. When they smiled, their teeth looked stained, because they chewed beetle nut, believing that black teeth were beautiful. Their dark hair hung in twisted strands, flowing over the naked babies that they held. Little children clung onto their mothers' hips or watched from behind the row of men.

Traveling at about 35 mph, Gibbs reached a ditch and pressed the brake to slow the VTR, but the tracks locked, and the tank slammed to a stop. I got flung forward, clipping Gibbs along the side of his face, and landed on my back about 20 feet away. My lungs emptied, and I tried to take a breath in order to get off the path, thinking that the tank was going to run me over. While getting back onto my feet, I felt the burning in my left arm.

An explanation of the hold up got radioed through the convoy, and one of the medics ambled over, examined the injury, concluded that I had torn some muscles, and strapped my arm in a makeshift sling. The convoy continued onward.

When we got nearer to VC Valley, the two gun tanks and our VTR took off in a different direction. We kept following the gun tanks, which began going one way and then switched course.

Eventually the tanks halted, and a soldier handed a map to the two commanders, who then studied the topographical layout of mountains, rivers and valleys, glanced about the area and then looked back on the creased paper that had been spread on the back plate of the tank.

Sergeant Robinson got on the radio, and with an expression of increasing confusion, he and a sergeant from

Camp Enari headquarters tried to coordinate what was on the map with what Robinson described of the terrain from his location.

I was sitting on the VTR, my fingers feeling numb from the injury, when the commanders called me over, wanting to know if I remembered my map reading from training. I took the map and turned north, trying to figure out where we were and where we were supposed to be going. Something wasn't right.

The one commander explained that the Spanish priests had drawn the maps years ago, and the French and the Vietnamese had done the updating. I handed back the map to the commander, and we used a compass, the sun and common sense.

After rendezvousing with an infantry unit of about 35 soldiers, we continued to VC Valley, where we were given orders to park a gun tank on each side of the perimeter, with our VTR stationed to the left of one of the tanks.

In the cleared away area, the couple hundred infantry had dug trenches, with their ponchos stretched over the top on branches for shade.

A helicopter pilot maneuvered his chopper down, and three officers, shielding their eyes from the whirling dust, ducked under the blades and headed toward headquarters. When the chopper lifted, the gust ripped up the grunts' ponchos and scattered their boonie hats, shirts and socks that had been taken off to dry. The soldiers scrambled to hold down their ponchos and then gathered whatever the wind didn't swipe beyond the perimeter where retrieval was not worth the risk.

With the night, rifle fire echoed, and the shimmer of explosions hovered briefly within the distant darkness. The tank across from us fired one round for affect, intentionally further from exact coordinates. Corrections were radioed back, in order that when required, the tanker could hit exactly where the guys in the jungle needed.

The call came for white phosphorous, and the far tank rocked back, absorbing the recoil and then with a blast, a white aura engulfed the tank, lifted slowly into a haze and then settled onto the ground. The tank provided the artillery for about an hour, interspersing white phosphorous between high explosive rounds.

On our side of the perimeter, I rested on my usual place over the tank engine, my injured arm awkwardly against my chest. If the tank had to fire the main gun, I had ten seconds to get clear of the back deck.

When a soldier awoke me for guard duty, I crawled up to the turret in the commander's hatch, and positioned myself behind the machine gun. A .45 grease gun lay across my lap for any Vietcong who tried boarding the tank.

I peered into the darkness of the jungle, leaning forward with every slight sound, my fingers touching the cold barrel of the .45, while wondering how the group of grunts in the jungle would fare. I could feel the enemy watching...waiting.

The next day, Gibbs and Conrad took the VTR and began clearing the heavy brush and trees away within the perimeter. One of the gun tank crews asked me to fill in as loader, and we rolled out of camp, over the terrain, reaching a small village, where only a collection of rust colored chickens scurried amongst the soldiers' boots as the men searched the precariously propped up bamboo shacks twisted over with vines.

On our way to do recon in the next village, we crossed

paths with Gibbs and Conrad, their VTR caught on a log, the tracks rotating just above the ground. I told Gibbs that since he got the tank caught, he would have to get it loose, but I suggested that he try C-4. Conrad stood behind the .50 caliber, scanning the area. Gibbs glared at me from the driver's hatch. As our group pulled away in the gun tank, I could hear him cursing at me.

I learned later that the engineers had tried the C-4 explosive. Gibbs had stayed in the tank for the first attempt, the resonating boom nearly shattering his eardrums. With part of the tree yet lodged in the drive sprocket and the group of soldiers cussing about the predicament, the engineers tried again with the C-4, lifting the VTR off the ground and creating a hail of wood shrapnel.

The following day, Gibbs and Conrad attempted to knock down a tree with the VTR dozer blade. Gibbs backed up the tank about ten feet, shifted into forward, hit the gas hard and rammed the tree. A thick branch snapped back, catching Conrad in the chest, yanking him from the hatch. He tumbled over the deck and landed with a thud onto the ground. The medics came out, waited until he was breathing properly and told him to get back to work.

Conrad dusted himself off and slowly climbed back up onto the tank while blaming Gibbs for what he believed was a deliberate accident. Gibbs let Conrad know what he thought of that accusation, and they then drove off outside the perimeter to clear away another area.

I got called out later that evening because the VTR had thrown a track. With daylight fading, the tank became a crippled metal target in enemy territory.

We decided to break apart the track in order to get it correctly aligned. Big Paul Callahan, a soldier from the gun tank, leaned down on the breaker bar, loosening the bolts.

Conrad dragged the partially assembled track sections out of the back of a deuce and a half truck. After connecting the extra track, seven soldiers strained against the 800 pounds of limp, buckling steel, trying to lift the track sections high enough to pull over the rear sprocket wheel.

I had taken off my sling, and the torn muscles in my arm throbbed, numbing my fingers, though the pain felt inconsequential compared to what I knew...the VC were watching and waiting.

The soldiers from the gun tank understood that their priority was with the LZ, but they also understood that if they left us without a working tank, Gibbs, Conrad and I would be dead by morning. We needed the gun tank soldiers. We needed Callahan. I repositioned the guys along the length of the track for one last try.

Except for our rigorous breathing, we worked quietly, our eyes darting over the dimming landscape, sweat running down our faces, our boots slipping against the ground, and the red grit from the track scraping across our arms and chests. With every minute lost, the enemy claimed the land like a black shroud, and our collected urgency became a force of focused adrenaline.

With the effort of the other soldiers, Callahan worked relentlessly, hoisting the track sections over his arm and charging forward, his bare back and shoulders bent under the weight, every muscle tight and controlled as if he had summoned all of his exceptional strength against the fate of that place.

Then the track clanked heavily over the sprockets. Gibbs put the tank into forward gear and walked the track on.

Callahan glanced at Gibbs and me and then into the

darkness, his expression tense. He and his men then loaded up into their tank and began back.

While Conrad kept watch behind the .50 caliber, Gibbs and I proceeded to do what we had done countless times before, removing the slack of track and bolting both ends together, but on that day, and in that place, we worked frantically between the hour of life and death.

When the three of us finally crawled into our tank, the quiet of the approaching night felt different with the realization and relief that we had survived another day.

I believe Paul Callahan's strength saved us that night, because even as we rode back towards the LZ, we knew that the enemy was watching.

FOLLOWED BY A REQUIEM

Only an eclipsed path of light spared Donald Burch from complete blackness. With his boot pressing against a paddle, and scuffing his palms and knees, he crawled forward over the rough, sloping surface until he figured that he had found a good place to begin.

He leaned against the curved wall at a slightly teetering angle, retrieved the hammer and sharpened chisel from his belt, and began a steady striking that created a clanging that echoed like the ringing of a dulled bell.

Jagged pieces smashed around his boots, while ashy dust showered over his hair and face, leaving the taste of grit in his mouth.

The sun blazed down, stilling the air within with a sweltering, suffocating heaviness, as the distinctive dank smell of concrete engulfed the dark enclosure as if a musty mine.

Wiping a dirty wrist across his brow, Burch altered his position, and then worked his way towards the back, caught in the haze of gray that burned his eyes. The oppressive reverberating trapped him in a distracting solitude, and the rising heat had his pants soaked against his skin and the dog tag chain hot against the back of his neck.

After a few hours, he returned the hammer and the chisel through his belt and began forward towards the now crescent light.

Beginning his tour as an Engineer for D Company at the Oasis felt like a fortunate turn of events and when working on hammering out the hardened concrete from the cement mixer, the steel barrel made for an adequate shield if the enemy attacked.

What do soldiers bring back from war? Our boys returned wearing their last pair of given boots, their dog tags and a requisitioned uniform, the embroidered patches indicating their name, rank, branch of service and unit insignia. They brought back an olive drab duffel bag securing their few belongings. They brought back pictures that never truly revealed the entirety of their stories. Our soldiers brought back their stories, but these images rarely left the sanctity of their thoughts.

With the churning of the barrel, the concrete slapping down with the rotations, Burch leaned against the back wheel fender. He had only a short time ago returned from an assignment at the Black Hawk Fire Base. During the day, he had operated the mixer, pouring down concrete for the eventual barracks to be built. During the night, he had gone on guard duty and recon with the other soldiers.

He had worked amongst those men for nearly two months, enough time to have remembered a few of their names, and enough time to have talked with more than a few of those men. He and the soldiers of Black Hawk had gained an understood camaraderie.

Word of the tragedy traveled quickly.

Black Hawk Fire Base had been overrun.

Burch concentrated on his work, trying to forget the soldiers with whom he had only a short time ago done guard duty. *Why had they died, while he lived?* The grief followed him like a gray haze. He should feel fortunate, and he did, but fortune balanced against guilt held little compensation.

What do soldiers bring back from war? Our soldiers brought back gratitude for having survived their tour. Our soldiers brought back guilt for having survived their tour. Unfounded guilt often times guided their choices, dimmed their happiness, destroyed their chances, and altered who they would have been if not for the gloom of war.

The clerk from the Oasis, on route for supplies, had told Burch what had happened. During the night, the barracks of his former Delta Company had gotten hit by a rocket. Perhaps the clerk had known further details, but Burch had not asked. He did not want to know. The less he knew, the easier he figured that he could avoid the emotion, but knowing less did not take away the truth. Not knowing the details had not taken away the emotion. Only for timing of being transferred had he been spared. *Why had they died, while he lived?* He should feel fortunate, but his fortune felt sharp and suffocating, and the death of those soldiers echoed in his thoughts like an oppressive reverberating clang. D Company had been his family, and war had taken his Brothers.

What do soldiers bring back from war? Our soldiers brought back intense emotions wrought by death day after day, the killing and the dying. Guilt, hopelessness, anger and overwhelming grief were appropriate emotions for what soldiers endured, and yet they felt as though they needed to keep quiet about the flashbacks and the nightmares and the depression, because war is war, and they were to have accepted the killing and the dying, the deaths of their Brothers.

According to the soldiers who had witnessed the accident, two scraper operators had been racing, ripping over the dirt, a plume of dust swirling like a fiery haze. The roar of the engines had been fierce, the two soldiers keeping their focus on the unavailing victory. One of the soldiers began slowing down, the scraper rebelling against his attempted halt.

The other driver kept going, his fingers folded tight upon the steering wheel, and an expression of exhilaration on his smudged face.

The edge of the cliff arrived too quickly.

The report of the incident had returned with the other engineers.

Burch's thoughts lingered on the unfortunate fate of a boy only his age, and the image of that soldier gripping the steering wheel, his uniform flapping against the uproar of air, and every muscle braced with the dire realization as he plunged over the cliff.

That soldier, like so many other boys, had been simply trying to forget, for even the slightest of time, the realities of war that rattled his resilience. With the speed of the scraper, for the slightest of time, that soldier had found a way to feel powerful and fearless, privileges of youth that he had nearly forgotten in Nam, yet with one error fraught with the innocence of youth, he had died.

What do soldiers bring back from war? Our boys brought

back a confusion acquired from the confines of war, rules that only applied to battles, discipline that appeared to have lost direction and military training that constantly clashed with the realities of home. They brought back conclusions that lacked logic and perceptions altered by suffering. They brought back vigilance, caution and quick defense, and yet those necessary survival tactics of war became like punishments of paranoia when they returned home.

The truth arrived at Camp Enari, and then drifted amongst the men like a heavy gray fog. The mixer barrel rumbled in a repetitious beat that Burch barely noticed. He had been at Dak To on the night of the attack. When the mortars began exploding across the base, he had taken position under the gun truck, behind the front dual tires, the cooling steel axle over his shoulder, and his M-16 aimed towards the perimeter. Rifle fire had sparked in the darkness, while tracer rounds lingered an aura of light. An uneasy intensity had settled over Dak To. Throughout the night, he had kept vigilant for possible approaching enemy, the thwacking beat of the eventual arriving gun ships like a distant steady striking in the dim sky.

With the quiet of the morning, soldiers returned from the perimeter, weary expressions and little conversation. With the light of the morning, Burch and the rest of the convoy had the opportunity to return to Camp Enari.

He had exited Dak To without really knowing. He had hoped that he would never really know, but tragedy in war cannot be kept quiet. The guys along the perimeter had suffered injuries and deaths amongst their men, and those who survived would forever feel the loss.

Like every soldier, Burch wanted to keep his Brothers

protected, but war is war, and he was to have accepted the killing and the dying, but he could not accept so much dying, and the trapped emotions held him in a grievous solitude.

What do soldiers bring back from war? Our soldiers brought back beliefs of blame, often times from the unavoidable consequences of a grim war. They brought back shifted expectations that failed to halt the images of Nam at night and dulled what felt like futile days, for they were now forever soldiers, with years of youth irretrievably lost. Our boys brought back the names of their Brothers, names that sometimes faded, leaving only hazy images, or names they kept secure with quiet reverence.

The gray rolled like a slow wave, crashing down, yet Burch invited the empty feeling, if only for the emptiness to ease his anguish.

They had died. He had lived.

He felt anger towards the war. He felt guilty for surviving. He felt alone in his tragedy. He felt overwhelming grief for the loss of those soldiers.

There existed no fortunate end in war.

They had been north of Kontum, E Company's 4th Squad, assembling a bridge during the day, as the scorching sun lashed down upon their backs. During the night, they had taken turns on watch, the distant cracks of rifle fire colliding with their few hours of allotted sleep. The weariness had weighed upon them, an internal struggle that seeped away their physical and emotional strength.

Burch remembered standing with three other guys, holding up part of the bridge, waiting for their next order.

He remembered the blank expressions of those three soldiers, as if their thoughts had been scattered and numbed by exhaustion. They stood beneath the bridge portion, their muscles locked in stance.

The usual clamor of the engineers had lured Burch's thoughts into a calm nothingness. He awoke with a jerk, his shoulders and curled fingers stiffening, and the three other soldiers noting the situation without judgment.

During the following days, the enemy continued to approach, the bursts of their AK-47s flashing in the darkness of the jungle.

A group of grunts were positioned between the jungle and the river, while the 4th Squad had been working across the river, their perimeter defense reflecting the briefness of their assignment. Concertina wire had been strung around the small area, a few claymore mines strategically placed, and during the night a soldier had been kept ready on the gun truck, firing off so many tracer rounds that the barrel of the right gun eventually melted.

A sergeant sent Burch by chopper to the nearest fire base to find a replacement. The search had proven futile, and with the waiting for further information, Burch had sat down against the sand bags and fallen asleep.

At three o'clock in the morning, he had been awoken by one of the soldiers of the base and told that a chopper had arrived to take him back. He would be transferred to the 2nd Squad.

With the gears of the mixer grinding in a hollow bellow, Burch tried, to no avail, to distract the thoughts that created images of what had happened to his 4th Squad while he had been at the fire base.

One of the claymore mines had been turned around.

When a soldier hit the clacker trigger, the arc of shrapnel blasted back into their perimeter, slicing and tearing and ripping through the soldiers. Burch knew enough about the destruction of claymore mines. Within that instant, shocked bewilderment would have quickly become gasps of panic, cries of pain and the silence of death.

Despite Burch's effort to block the truth, he could not escape the images of the men of E Company 4th Squad lying on the ground, blotches of blood seeping and spreading across their uniforms, their expressions breaking with fear.

They would have attempted to stop the bleeding, and if unable, they would have waited, while praying that they were not dying. They would have hoped that the other wounded men were being helped, while dreading the eventual arriving knowledge of the list of those who had died…the soldiers who were silent, fallen upon their M-16s, their helmet straps yanked against their necks, their faces cradled in the dirt.

What do soldiers bring back from war? What do soldiers give? Our boys gave of their courage, even when they were afraid. They gave of their strength, even when they were exhausted. They gave of their hope, even when the darkness appeared hopeless. They gave of their loyalty, even when their Brothers kept dying. What did our soldiers sacrifice for the war? They sacrificed more than what can be told in their stories.

THE RAIN

For whom in war should we weep? Should we weep for the soldiers who died in an instant, without time to understand? Should we weep for the soldiers who were wounded, suffering and afraid, knowing that they could not escape death? Do we weep for the wives and brothers and sisters and mothers and fathers and friends who waited, only, in the end, to be told with terse military protocol that their soldiers had died? Or do we weep for the boys who lived…soldiers who heard the ragged, panicked gasps…soldiers who returned home with far less than what they gave…soldiers who remember all the tragic things of war that the dead have long forgotten?

Gibbs and I were given orders to join a convoy north of Pleiku, traveling towards Kontum, where we would be repairing a mine roller. We fueled up the War Wagon, checked the .50 caliber machine gun, ammo and the foot locker for an adequate supply of LAW rockets and collected our quota of C rations and malaria tablets. The next morning I made my way to the Tank Park, where Gibbs was already waiting, started the 12 cylinder engine, and we exited Camp Enari.

After about a half hour, we reached Pleiku and took our place last in line in the 40 vehicle convoy, which included a deuce and a half truck transporting infantry, an armored vehicle, flat bed trucks hauling supplies, three-quarter ton pickup type vehicles and jeeps with mounted M-60 machine guns. The lead jeep had a grooved metal post welded to the front grill that could cut wire if strung across the road by the enemy, a device intended to slice our throats.

The convoy rumbled over the steep mountain roads at about 35 mph, slowing on the up rise of the slopes and gaining speed when going down. Jets streaked through the sky, leaving a trail of wispy white, helicopters arched across the blue and occasionally a low flying cargo plane would rumble over, spraying the jungle with a heavy haze.

At the base camp before Kontum, most of the convoy pulled off in a different direction. Gibbs and I kept going until we reached the bridge bordering the city, where a few of our men were on guard duty.

We worked on the damaged tank roller. I tugged the chain over the dirt, hooked it to the broken bar, and Gibbs eased the VTR forward, trying to get the jammed torsion bar loose. Our efforts failed.

That night we pulled guard duty with some of the soldiers by the bridge. A tank had been parked on each end, and a search light flashed back and forth. I slept in a bunker, hearing the pounding of distant battles as a glow from explosions and tracer rounds illuminated the sky. After a few hours of ineffective sleep, I took my hours at watch, waiting for my chance to return to the bunker.

The next morning, I went out to one of the gun tanks and cooked my C ration and a pack of hot chocolate. Gibbs and I then got back to the roller but had no better luck loosening the torsion bar. I decided to try C-4 on the back of the bar and unscrewed the top of a hand grenade, inserted the blasting cap into the C-4, pulled the pin and counted the seven seconds as I walked around to the other side of the tank.

Kontum base camp heard the blast and thought the bridge was under attack. Their RTO was on the radio demanding to know our status, and I explained to him that I had simply derived the most efficient route for releasing a jammed torsion bar.

The Camp Enari sergeant was informed and not pleased. Our conversation consisted of a reminder of military regulations, with the inclusion of his cursing and my promise to never blow anything up again without radioing him first.

A few days later the parts arrived. Gibbs and I finished fixing the mine roller and followed the roller tank across the bridge and through Kontum.

Within the city of Kontum, a ten foot brick wall had been built around a large beige building with a center steeple and wooden shutters over rows of windows. On the porch stood orphaned Vietnamese children wearing loin cloths or naked in the hot sun, watching our tank with vacant eyes under disheveled black hair. Little girls huddled together, and the boys braved their way towards the wall whispering words that we couldn't understand. I tossed over some C rations, but the missionary women snatched up the cans before the kids could get any.

I learned later that the food U.S. soldiers intended for the children ended up being given to the Vietcong. I didn't throw C rations over the wall again.

During my tour in Vietnam, I would pass the orphanage countless times. Eventually I could look at a kid and know about how long he or she had left before disappearing from the flow of orphans. These kids died slowly, their dark eyes desperate, like they understood that they were considered merely rubbish of the war. We watched children die and could do nothing.

Gibbs and I continued out of town, climbed a steep embankment and then went north a few *klicks*, reaching our destination. The soldiers lowered the roller and drove slowly over the dirt road, hoping to disengage any explosives missed by the mine sweep guys. These soldiers with hand mine detectors were further in front, earphones on, gliding the detectors back and forth.

The guys on the gun tank told us stories about soldiers who had stepped on an explosive, tearing and tossing those soldiers in a rain of red dirt and blood. Once the dust had settled, those who gathered around the tattered body had a mere moment to honor their Brother before getting back to war.

To reach the pontoon bridge, we followed the dirt roads towards the mountain, with ledges sometimes dropping 40 feet down. The *bridge apes* had a good number of soldiers at the bunker and guard post on our side. An infantry unit guarded the other side of the bridge. These soldiers, living in their trenches and sand bag bunkers, had filthy uniforms, burned faces, and when we talked with them, their red rimmed eyes and short replies indicated their weary resignation to their dire fate.

The next day, Gibbs and I, along with a new guy who wanted to be on a tank crew, went again towards Kontum to retrieve another broken down tank. We hooked up the damaged tank and began back, crossed a river but got stuck on the rising embankment. We tried to maneuver the VTR and the towed tank, but our engine was losing power. Fortunately, another tank arrived and pulled us loose. We towed the damaged tank back to Kontum base camp but couldn't begin the repairs until the ordered engine arrived. The three of us decided to go back to the bridge for the night.

I drove the War Wagon hard, hoping for a few hours of sleep, but as we neared, a soldier ran towards us. Our tank radio wasn't working, and the guys at Kontum couldn't reach us, but they had radioed over to our guys by the bridge that a convoy had been hit, yet taking sniper fire, and a soldier was trapped in a blown up vehicle.

I turned the tank around and began back in full throttle. The speed, rough road and abrupt turns in my effort to avoid the two foot deep ruts in the road pummeled the new guy against the rigger hatch. I slowed down, but Gibbs looked at me with his commanding expression and told me, *you drive; we ride when lives are at stake*. I took the tank to full speed.

When we reached the convoy, the night was already nearing. Gibbs positioned the machine gun and sprayed the tree line with bullets. I got the torch, pulled goggles over my eyes and let the blue flame chew through the metal. Fire crackled into a shower of gold rain and the smell of seared steel fogged in my face. A protective shield had been slid between my torch work and the soldier caught in the wreckage. He was slumped against the crushed truck frame, the medics having already loaded him with morphine. When I had burned through enough to get him loose, the medics took over.

Gibbs repositioned the VTR and used the boom to lift one of the other vehicles. The War Wagon sunk into the soft dirt and the right track came part way off. The convoy continued onward, and we were stranded in enemy territory without a working tank.

We took the end connectors off and attempted to walk the track back on, only for the edge to catch crooked and slip off again. We worked quietly, with an occasional curse, our muscles straining with the heavy track. Eventually, we decided that we had to get going before the Vietcong discovered our predicament.

Gibbs limped the tank along with the new guy behind the .50 caliber, while I walked in front, gripping the M-16, my finger on the trigger, watching for the VC and looking for mines on a road obscured by darkness. I used the grind of the tank engine to gauge how close I kept to the tracks.

Then the rain came, dripping down my hair, splashing into my eyes. Before long, my uniform was drenched, and my boots were filled with cold water, my feet raw against the grimy soles as the strings tightened against my ankles.

Gibbs maneuvered the tank, while keeping watch of where I was walking. The new guy clung onto the machine gun, only loosening his hold when he wiped the rain from his glasses.

If the Vietcong attacked, the plan was for me to throw myself onto the tank blade, and then Gibbs would try to outrun the ambush. If I didn't reach the blade, Gibbs would figure that I was dead.

I walked for what felt like hours, shivering from the cool night air seeping through my wet clothes. My feet stumbled over the sloppy road, and my thoughts created shadows that my blurred vision could not decipher.

Finally we reached a landing zone. I climbed in the tank and the three of us crawled into our wet sleeping bags. My skin itched with the soaked, dirty uniform, my feet ached in the wet canvas boots, and an odor like rotting warm jungle rose like steam from my sleeping bag…but I didn't care.

Two hours later I bolted upward. An officer had come to tell us that he didn't appreciate tankers arriving late at night without his zone being notified. He wanted us gone as soon as possible, because he knew the enemy targeted mechanics.

We had breakfast, went to work and after a few hours, repaired the track. With the tank low on fuel, we stopped at the Kontum base. They agreed to give us 150 gallons of their limited fuel supply if we agreed to pull back one of their broken down vehicles.

By the time we reached the VTR, the day had dimmed to gray. The two stranded soldiers kept low in their tank, having earlier contended with sniper fire. Gibbs shot off a few rounds to back off any lingering snipers and to ease the fear of the two VTR soldiers. The one soldier had his arm in a makeshift sling and a few red soaked bandages. The other soldier had no apparent injuries, but both of them kept quiet, their attention rattled by the noises of the approaching night, and their eyes following the progress of our work. We were all tired and understood the balance of pride and gratitude.

We towed them back, and because their base camp was expecting an attack, we decided to stay for the night. There had been reports of Vietcong within the wire and a considerable force waiting just beyond.

With the darkness, a soldier hurried over, clutching his M-16, glancing around, talking fast, and his finger twitching near the trigger. He claimed that the enemy had the camp surrounded. He claimed that he saw the whites of their eyes.

I told him that the darkness could be deceiving, but he shook his head, and insisted that the Vietcong were waiting. I went with him to the east perimeter and peered into the blackness. With his rifle shaking and aimed at the trees, he kept whispering about how he had *nips in the wire*. We waited awhile without incident, and he eventually calmed down. I returned to the tank.

That night I had guard duty, and when I finally had a chance to sleep, I slept sitting up in the tank's loader seat with my knees cramped against my chest. The quiet of the night lured my dreams towards the edge of wariness, and when I awoke, it was as if the night had never happened.

The next day, I put the engine in the other tank and ended up again on guard duty. Physically, I kept alert, capable, but the lack of sleep began blurring my thinking.

The following day, we joined the convoy going back to Pleiku. The War Wagon's engine surged and jerked when we tried to gain speed. By the time we reached Camp Enari, we were traveling about three miles per hour, with the rest of the convoy having long before crossed through the gate.

The new guy crawled out of the tank, abandoning what should have been a four-man crew, and walked away. The risks apparently did not coincide with his hopes of surviving the war.

I started dismantling the engine and didn't quit until it was too dark to work. The next day, I returned to the Tank Park. A soldier from the Motor Pool with a wrecker helped lift out the engine, and we hauled it over to supplies.

The supply building was only a few yards away from Graves Registration, a Quonset hut with a refrigeration area in the back. Those who worked for Graves Registration were responsible for getting bodies ready for shipping back home.

Day after day, those working within that building sorted through the tattered bodies of boys. They cut off boots and rotting uniforms, often times finding creased, faded photos.

They touched shattered faces. They lived amongst the dead, in order to verify the name of each soldier, knowing that their accuracy would spare unknown families, while bringing an inconsolable tragedy for others.

In the back of an army truck parked at the entrance of Graves Registration were dead soldiers in body bags. The bodies were stacked on top of each other, three or four high above the tailgate. Two soldiers hoisted down the black bags and walked with shuffling steps, trying to keep the weight of the body from dragging. They kept their glances forward, not wanting to focus on what they were carrying.

I didn't want to watch, but the image of those soldiers piled in a suffocating heap held me for a moment. I wondered how it felt to be dead, silent on a cold metal table, uniform cut off, dog tags unhooked from around my neck.

How does war deceive so many boys and hide the truth in black bags?

I think that it would have been better to have seen the truth of death. I think that while watching such a grievous scene it would have been better to have cried, but soldiers don't cry if they want to survive.

We got our engine and returned back to camp. That night I went on guard duty. We got to our bunkers and decided who went on what watch. I kept the detonator for the claymore mines near me and called in every hour to assure the sergeant of the guard that everything was OK. Standing quietly, I watched the darkness shift and change with my imagination partly caught in the war and partly thinking about my family.

Eventually the next soldier took his turn, nudging me on the shoulder, his weary expression obscured by his helmet. I crawled onto the cot, a deep exhaustion trying to drag away the endlessness of war.

During the night a rat scurried over me. I waited for the poisonous snake that usually followed, and when nothing happened, I fell back into a restless sleep, with every sound having my hand quick on the rifle.

The next day, I tried again on the engine. Without a muffler, the tank's rumble could be heard throughout camp. Just when I thought that I had almost fixed the problem, the sergeant showed up, agitated by the racket and ordered me back to the supply station to get a different engine.

War does not halt for broken down tanks, or abandoned children, or soldiers without enough sleep. The Vietnam War did not end when soldiers stepped on explosives or when entire platoons were destroyed, or when rescue helicopters crashed. The War did not halt for years of tears like an endless rain. The Vietnam War kept reigning until over 58,000 U.S. soldiers died.

I drove back to the supply station. Another truck waited at Graves Registration.

How We Went Home

Our waitress wore a short red skirt. She had soft brown eyes, shiny black hair that brushed upon her shoulders and a shy smile as she served me and the Clerk cold beer with breakfast at the Air Force Club. Other soldiers were sitting by the bar or at the dark cloth covered round tables. A hazy curtain of smoke obscured the lights, while music clanged from the jukebox. I could almost forget that I was in the middle of a war. . .almost.

The camp Clerk had asked me the day before if I wanted to go with him, and since he promised to be able to get the proper paper work and a jeep, I agreed. We stayed through lunch, talking about our life before Nam and playing tic-tac-toe with the waitresses.

About two o'clock, we began back, the Clerk driving. He turned off the main road, explaining that he wanted to stop at the Oasis, in that he knew a few guys who were stationed at that base.

After passing the checkpoint, I pulled out my .45 and took target practice at rocks and tin cans in the ditch. The hum of the jeep with the occasional crack of a bullet against the gravel felt like a good end to a good day.

I had gone through a few clips when the Clerk asked if I would drive. We stopped, I tossed my .45 into the back of the jeep, and we exchanged places.

He reached over, brought my gun to the front, loaded

one round and laid the .45 across his lap, his hand lightly on the barrel. I drove while he sat quietly. His eyes were watching the road in front of us, but he wasn't focusing on the road, only whatever internal predicament he was trying to resolve.

He pulled the trigger.

The bullet went through his knee, and then between my right leg and the gas pedal.

I turned and asked him, *what the hell are you doing?!*

He just sat there with an expression torn between guilt and relief. I threw the .45 once again into the back seat and stepped down on the gas.

When pain replaced the numbness, the Clerk pleaded for morphine as he rocked forward, his hands clasped over his knee, and his pants soaked with red. I kept my concentration on the road, and told him that we had no morphine.

Another jeep was on the road further in front, and as we approached, I pressed on the horn, but they didn't hear, so I decided to pass on the right.

Just as my front fender cleared the back of their jeep, the driver noticed us and swerved. The jeeps collided, and we went off a 15 foot embankment at 45 miles per hour.

Both the Clerk and I were thrown from the vehicle. I didn't remember hitting the ground, but when I regained consciousness, I could see the Clerk lying not far from me, and I pulled myself over by him.

The guys from the other jeep worked their way down the steep slope, trying to keep balance on the loose dirt. Turns out they were medics returning from Pleiku. They gave the Clerk a shot of morphine, and I think they gave me something, because everything suddenly went black. I awoke with the thwacking of helicopter blades, the air rushing against me while a medic leaned over, stuck me with a needle and the medic and the chopper faded.

I couldn't understand what they were saying, hushed voices deciding what to do with me. I was surrounded, couldn't move and without my gun. I waited for the crack of an AK-47 to put a bullet through my head.

Then I recognized one of the voices. . .the Clerk telling me that everything was going to be OK. I opened my eyes. The bright lights seemed to sway over me, while a nurse sliced through my pants, pulling the fabric away piece by piece as the doctor cut off my boots with a sharp short bladed surgical scissors.

He told me that I was probably paralyzed from the waist down. I told him *bullshit*, grabbed the edge of the table, and swung my feet onto the floor. My knees buckled, and the nurses caught me and hoisted me again onto the table. While they worked on the Clerk, I lay on my back, shivering on the cold stainless steel.

Eventually, with the assistance of a nurse, I slowly lowered myself from the table and stood briefly. The nurse gave me some clothes and boots that didn't fit, and then with a wheelchair, took me to another ward and helped me onto a bunk.

The next morning, I felt like I had been trampled. Each slight movement to get off the bed made me stop and shudder as the pain struck, lingered and then slowly subsided until I moved again. Once on my feet, I limped along, briefly halting when my vision dimmed, and I would close my eyes and wait until the room stopped teetering before continuing down the corridor and through the double doors.

I found the Clerk and talked with him. He would be

going home with broken bones, a shattered knee and the knowledge of a decision planned with desperation.

As I shuffled into the other rooms, I saw a part of war not easily forgotten. . .young soldiers broken far beyond repair. I held up a glass of water for a soldier without arms, putting the straw into his mouth. Another soldier near him asked if I could do the same. I got a soldier his bedpan. He had no legs. I helped him, and then put the bedpan on the floor where a nurse could empty it when she had time.

These soldiers asked for help with quiet voices humbled by their compassion for every other soldier struggling with them. They were no longer the innocent boys who had landed in Vietnam, but brave, hardened men who had seen agony and death and the shattering of their own once powerful youth. They now needed to believe that being spared from death, they had to find the power to return home as different men.

Within that hospital I saw soldiers with their ears or noses or jaws torn apart from explosives. . .jagged, red scars cutting across once pure faces. I stood in the room of a soldier who sat staring into nothing. . .not hearing, not knowing, lost in emptiness. I wondered who would be waiting for him. Who would help him and all those other soldiers?

My injuries and my pain seemed suddenly incidental. The sacrifices of these soldiers could not be compensated, but I could honor their sacrifice by standing with my Brothers in battle. The next day, without the doctor's consent, I hitched a ride back to base.

We came to Vietnam as young, rugged, resilient boys, not knowing enough…not knowing nearly enough, but we went home without legs to walk off the plane or arms to embrace our families. We went home with burned bodies, altered emotions and grievous images that we yet cannot escape. How can we *forget* the war, when this is how we went home?

Of Courage and Sacrifice

Robert L. Moneypenny had been drafted into the army. Following basic training and advanced infantry training, he volunteered for Vietnam, where he became an Armored Vehicle Launch Bridge Commander of the 4th Engineers, E Company Armor Platoon. He figured that one of two possible outcomes awaited him. He could, perhaps, return home a hero, a premise upon which he hoped to alter the discouragement that had befallen him nearly a year prior, or he would end up dead, which, at the time, felt appropriately rebellious towards a God whom he believed had betrayed his faithfulness. At 19, the circumstances in his life had brought loneliness, and the actuality of his own end appeared unlikely, but when he entered Nam, he discovered that in war, very little separated truth and illusion, loneliness and love, fear from faith, and life from death.

A shrill whistling tore through the dimming evening sky. Moneypenny knew the sound, the distinct decreasing pitch, and the reverberating tremor indicating near proximity. Clutching his M-16, he began running towards the bunker, adrenaline surging, propelling him forward in wild bounds.

During the last ten months he had endured enemy attacks and sniper fire, but now, with only 65 days left of his tour, he suddenly understood the gravity of his nonchalant acceptance of his own mortality amid wavering spiritual beliefs. The idea of dying had been easier to disregard before an incoming mortar was streaking down directly onto his path. He did not want to be hauled away in a body bag. He did not yet welcome the end.

In a flood of emotions and memories, his thoughts became focused on the one Power capable of sparing him, and he gave a last desperate request. *Oh God, I didn't really mean I wanted to die.*

The whistling became louder, a dull, heavy, hollow sound. Moneypenny dove, impacting the ground with panicked force, his face scraping against the dirt, his rifle, held in his left fist, caught tight under his chest.

He heard the mortar strike with an eerie finality, seemingly silencing the earth and numbing his body. He waited for the explosion. He waited for the pain. He waited for the feeling of death, hoping to get past the inevitable pain. He waited second by second, wondering if his 19 years had been worthy or worthwhile. He waited, but nothing happened.

With his right arm yet shielding his face, Moneypenny glanced up, releasing the air that had been trapped in his lungs. The mortar lay on the ground five feet to his left, resembling the miniature bombs with squared back fins once dropped from WWII Bombers. Moneypenny stared at the mortar with a disoriented disbelief, like noting the oddity of a vicious creature suddenly turned docile.

He pushed himself up onto his knees while keeping suspicious watch of the explosive and then crawled onto his feet. Cautiously he backed away a few steps and then charged towards the bunker.

Bullets struck the stacked sand bags, sinking through the

canvas and creating wisps of dust. An officer and another soldier were positioned next to the bunker gun port, daring quick glances. Moneypenny joined them, surveying the perimeter in an effort to locate the sniper, perhaps the same Vietcong responsible for the mortar. A fourth soldier stood further towards the back, both hands gripping his M-16.

A few moments later, three other soldiers rushed into the bunker. Two of these boys took towards the back, their breathing heavy and erratic. The third soldier, rugged in stature, blond hair, blue eyes and bronzed from the sun, leaned against the wall near Moneypenny. With the ping of the bullets striking the tin, this rugged soldier's jaw tightened, his voice sounding raspy, *Oh God, keep us safe. I go home in seven days.*

This soldier, when he had first entered the war, had contended with, and eventually conquered the panic that every new soldier experienced. He had during the course of time accepted a dreary fate, replacing futile emotions with daring risks, but now with the graspable chance of surviving Nam, his expression held both the fading hope of going home and a fervent determination restrained by cautious defense. Despite an earlier ambivalence to death, now, with only seven days remaining of his tour, he did not want to be hauled away in a body bag. He did not yet welcome the end.

Moneypenny, the officer and the soldiers near the gun port perceived the apparent assault as a single sniper waging harassment fire, yet the three soldiers sitting tight against the back corner, shuddered every time a bullet hit the bunker. They yanked out their ammunition clips, checking that each was properly loaded, and then returned the clips carefully back to their bandoliers, slightly above the flap for quick retrieval. Their eyes darted with the shadows of the dimming sky, and they held their M-16s with the awkward inexperience of boys who had never handled a weapon prior to basic training, and who had never needed to ready a rifle against an enemy.

The officer went over by these three new soldiers and told them that the bunker would protect them if they stayed inside. In a casual tone he added that the lone sniper was a lousy shot. One of the soldiers standing near the gun port reminded the new soldiers that they were all Brothers, and Brothers took care of each other.

War offered no promises, no deliverance, but the camaraderie amongst soldiers, forged within the months of trials and weariness, the days of chaos and loneliness, the hours of fear and faith and the moments of love and pure grief for their Brothers, offered the only hope. Soldiers kept emotions hidden, but of their courage and devotion, the risking of their lives for each other, of these tributes they gave until the end.

After a half hour, the sniper fire ceased. The officer turned towards the six soldiers and told them that information had been received earlier through intelligence from the observation of air recon that a considerable company of Vietcong was approaching the camp. He told them that they better be prepared to fight.

The new soldiers paled. The idea of dying on that day had been easier to disregard before knowing that a company of Vietcong was approaching the camp.

Moneypenny asked the soldier standing next to him if he was OK.

Clutching his rifle, this boy named Thomas nodded and replied, *I am a U. S. soldier, here to serve my country.*

With his sinewy build, dark hair and brown eyes,

Thomas reminded Moneypenny of a friend he knew back home, and an unexplained feeling prompted Moneypenny to approach the officer, requesting that the new in country be teamed with a battled experienced man, further requesting that Thomas be teamed with him to feed the rounds into the machine gun. The officer agreed and then proceeded to alert the rest of camp to ready for the attack.

Moneypenny and Thomas gathered up their helmets, flak jackets, grenades and plenty of ammunition. In accordance with the officer's orders, Moneypenny secured the .30 caliber from his AVLB and positioned the machine gun within the trench at the center of the perimeter, while Thomas knelt beside him, watching intensely.

Three Phantom jets streaked over, firing rockets, the lingering haze of the explosions twisting down the distant mountain of Dak To.

In the quiet of the fading light, both boys, sitting side by side against the dirt of the trench, understood that the other would perhaps be allotted their last conversation.

Thomas reached under his flak jacket into his pocket and pulled out a small bible that his mother had given him when he had been drafted. Slowly he unzipped the black leather and turned the cover. The moon's glow reflected off the sheen from a silver plate with an engraved cross.

Moneypenny asked what was written below the cross. Thomas tipped back his helmet and recited the verse of Exodus 33:14. *My presence shall go with thee.*

Lightly tapping his fingers on the opposite page, he then indicated the scripted note written by his mother. What had been written could not be read within the blackness of the night, but Thomas knew the gift he kept against his heart, and whispered the words. *To my loving son Thomas, come home safely.*

He then looked down at the bible he held in the palm of his hand, carefully closed the cover, returned the book to his left army fatigue pocket and stared out over the trench into the darkness. He knew the inevitable could not be altered.

With both hands on the .30 caliber machine gun, Moneypenny peered out into the emptiness with an unwavering vigilance, his muscles twitching with the illusions of the night. He could hear the slow, steady breathing of the soldier next to him. He could feel in the cold quiet, the tense anticipation of a camp of soldiers bracing for battle.

On that night, Moneypenny wanted to believe in the God whom he had once trusted, but his faith felt far away, and within the trench, he understood his task as a soldier. He held the power of a .30 caliber machine gun. If the Vietcong attacked, he would use his training and instinct and weapon for the sake of himself, for Thomas and every other soldier in camp.

The existence of God. . .the destruction of war, how does a soldier find a logic that allows for both? How does a soldier resolve the conflict of honoring his God with prayer while defending himself and his Brothers with a rifle? How does a soldier believe in the strength of his own goodness when thrown into a vast expanse of decisions that waited within an ethical nightmare?

Some soldiers endured their time in Nam by the light of their faith. Some soldiers who entered the war without a belief in God, returned home with the urgency to embrace the belief of eternity. Some soldiers trusted in their God while they trudged through the tragedies of war, and then, understandably, began questioning the compassion or even the existence of God. By the end of their tour, the despair of constant death had altered their reality like a fractured mirror reflecting back broken images of themselves and life. With time, some soldiers sought their God again with a respect and wisdom only gained through the valiant and lonely journey of a soldier.

Life requires arduous obligations, none more complicated or emotional than the path of soldiers, where benevolent actions of devotion clashed with such intensity. Life further requests that enlightenment be gained, none gained with such poignancy as for soldiers endeavoring together to survive.

War collected boys and required of them to defend or die. Neither choice appeared acceptably ethical. With or without justification, the Vietnam War entailed military strategies, rules, rank, victories and defeats, yet within the obligations of war, soldiers deliberately or unknowingly honored their God by their endurance, compassion, courage and sacrifice for each other.

Their endurance and courage continued when they returned home and struggled against the past. Their compassion and sacrifice remains evident by their loyalty towards their Brothers. Every soldier followed a significant path. . .a journey that offered a divine purpose, but began with the walk through a mortal hell.

Robert L. Moneypenny survived his tour in Nam, but not without the images and nightmares of war following him home. Within that darkness of despair, he sought the light of his faith with a respect and wisdom gained through his journey as a soldier. He found his God waiting his return.

TWELVE OUNCES

Death is not a simple equation. Soldiers died everyday in Nam, but nonetheless, death is not a simple equation. Does destiny, timing or purpose play a part?

Bullets struck, instantly ending one soldier's life, or veered a fraction further, balancing another soldier's fate within the time required for dustoff or the length of the delay because of enemy fire.

Explosives were launched, and if the distance proved accurate, then death depended on how seriously a soldier got sliced by shrapnel, or how quickly the medics could reach each of the injured before too much blood had streamed onto the earth.

One wrong step from the soldier walking point, and death became a consequence of proximity and position in the line.

All things considered, often times, death required the combination of circumstances happening together.

Perhaps believing that for each of our tours in Nam, there existed a destined beginning and end, regardless of our efforts to keep alive, would have given us a sense of acceptance and peace…but then again, when existence had become an agenda of survival, who the hell had time to think about destiny?

Billowing dust floated upward like dirty fog as Robinson's tank tracks churned over the road. Patrick Callahan, the driver, kept a steady pace that coincided with the three engineer soldiers walking in front, two of the soldiers swinging mine sweep detectors in wide arcs.

Positioned behind the tank, and keeping a respectable distance, followed a deuce and a half truck hauling 25 grunts, who were sitting along both sides of the bed and a few standing in the middle.

The dust mixed with the bright sun and heat, creating a powdery haze over the convoy. The infantry soldiers, wiping the sweat dripping from beneath their helmets, kept a casual grip on the rifles tilted over their shoulders as they leaned back, tossing frivolous comments at each other.

Then the road erupted under the tank, time seemingly slowed and blurred by the tumultuous boom and the grind of metal being challenged and twisted. The force flung the crew within, ripped off road wheels, broke the track and lifted a 52 ton tank off the ground. The tank lurched forward and then crashed back down like an avalanche.

The engineer soldiers dove onto the dirt, their M-16s yanked in front, as the tremor vibrated beneath them and through the air.

Two personnel carriers from further back in the convoy accelerated and slammed to a stop, one on each side of Robinson's tank, the gunners rattling off rounds on the .50 calibers, as a veil of dust visually isolated the groups of soldiers from each other.

Standing infantry had scrambled from the truck into the ditches, and those sitting along the side had swung around, their knees bashing against the truck's planks as they positioned their rifles over the edge.

When the convoy's constant crack of firing ceased, the soldiers peered into the tree line, watching for any movement in the green, while Robinson and Callahan crawled from the hatches. They walked around the tank, surmising the damage, snatching up the breaker bar, the tow chain and two foot wrench, gesturing at each other, because they couldn't hear beyond the throbbing ringing in their ears.

The damage was considerable to the tank. . .warped hull, bent fender, cracked road wheels, broken track. The tank crew suffered considerable damage to their hearing, but Robinson and Callahan turned towards the infantry who were clutching their rifles, their eyes locked on the jungle. That mine would have torn through the truck. . . torn through those 25 soldiers. Robinson and Callahan easily accepted the consequences of their tank rolling over a mine in order to spare the lives of 25 men.

A few months later, Robinson's tank hit another mine. Gibbs and I fired up the VTR, and with the engine roaring and a blue flame torching from our exhaust pipe, we passed the check point and followed the tank trail.

The broken down tank was stranded between Dragon Mountain and the Tea Plantation, an area owned by the French with acres of trees and dominated by a mansion style building with a red clay colored roof and white pillars lining the entrance.

I pulled up the VTR 50 feet from the front of the tank as a precaution against the Vietcong's typical second buried mine.

While Gibbs kept behind the .50 caliber, I gathered four cans of beer from the VTR foot locker and walked over by

Robinson's tank. Three road wheels had been broken off by the blast and the left track blown apart, leaving a length of bolted metal track lying flat on the ground.

Sergeant Robinson stayed in the hatch ready to fire the 90 mm. He wore his helmet and mouth piece for communication with the loader and the computer specialist below. I handed up three beers, and Robinson dropped two cans down for his men.

The driver had crawled from the tank, pacing in short steps, watching the jungle for snipers. His boots grated against the dirt as adrenaline surged through him. He kept talking, telling me what happened, how he had no indication…no indication of the buried mine, how the force had thundered under them, lifting the left side of the tank, scattering the crew inside. He thought the Vietcong were waiting. He thought that the detonation of the mine was the beginning of their end.

I gave the driver a beer and the church key can opener that I kept on the chain of my dog tags. His hands shook so badly that the triangular blade kept slipping off the rim. He tried to steady the can between his palm and chest, but his other hand trembled, and he couldn't keep the opener in one place long enough to press the blade down. I watched his efforts only briefly before I took the can and opened it for him. He nodded and tipped the can to his mouth, spilling half the beer down his shirt as he gulped down the rest.

The mine sweep expert arrived about a half hour later by jeep and pulled up in front of the VTR. Wearing an olive drab military hat and regular uniform, Walker strode to where the tank had been hit, lowered the mine detector to the trail and began sweeping the device across the ground like a pendulum in an easy, rhythmic motion, concentrating only on the area in front of him and where his own boots fell.

I leaned against the damaged gun tank, watching Walker's tedious pace. He began on the far right of the road, moving forward until he passed the tank and reached the blown mine. Then he turned in an arc and began back with the same steady steps, slightly overlapping the prior path until he reached his determined end line and then turned to go forward again.

When he reached the middle of the trail, he deviated to the left side and proceeded to follow a path back and forth, until only the area between the two tanks remained unchecked. Lowering the detector to the ground, he moved forward, back, forward, stopped by my boots and told me to step aside.

I told him that there was no second mine, and that he should let us hook up so that we could all get the hell out of there. He shook his head, and with a steady stare, told me to step aside.

I stepped aside.

Walker glided the detector over the ground, listening through the headset. He paused, moved the device slower, a few inches one way, then the other, hovering over the area, his expression tense with listening. . .and I knew.

He glanced up at me, and I stood there looking at my boot prints directly on top of the second buried mine.

Walker, the sergeant and an officer got down on their knees and with their bayonets, slowly dug away the dirt from the mine's edges and then lifted the explosive from the ground. The mine had a 220 pound pressure plate.

When the mine had been removed from the road, I backed up the VTR to the gun tank and dropped the tow bar.

With a thud, the bar landed exactly where the mine had been buried. The weight of the bar would have set off the mine, and I would have been dead.

Soldiers walked on a blade of mortality, feeling death so near, breathing down their necks, but also feeling life so vividly when a day ended and they had not died. Death cannot be a simple equation when a soldier survives, despite standing on a buried mine, or a tank crew's position in a convoy spares the lives of 25 infantry. Death cannot be explained any better than the complicated truths of life. In war, only gratitude remained simple, understood between soldiers by a slight nod or fleeting expression or the offering and accepting of a 12 ounce can of beer.

THE CONSEQUENCE OF SURVIVAL

The Water Point, located a quarter of a mile beyond the perimeter of the Oasis base, consisted of an isolated bunker with a guard post on top, a few tanks, and with the frequent attacks, an insufficient number of soldiers.

The soldiers of the Water Point had disengaged the worn track of a gun tank, the 80 pads now lying flat beneath the tank's six road wheels, and were in the process of assembling the new track. A sergeant hauled the sections in the back of a jeep, while the other soldiers held ready sockets and wrenches to fasten the end connectors. When the completed length of the rubber coated steel track stretched across the ground, a soldier guided the tank driver as he rolled in reverse. With the directing soldier's held up fists, the driver halted, locking both sprockets, leaving nine feet of 28 inch wide track to be lifted over the right rear sprocket, approximately four and a half feet off the ground.

Nineteen year old Thomas Vojvodich and two other men grabbed the five foot pry bars from the sponson box and jammed the tapered end into the dirt, using the leverage to heave the weight of the track upward. The other three soldiers plowed forward with the thick metal like a harness across their forearms.

The track was stiff and unyielding, resisting the bend, and only the brute strength of the six men forced the nearly 1000 pound portion of track slowly into place over the 27 and a half inch diameter rear drive sprocket.

For the sake of alignment, the men slightly shifted their forward momentum. The track lurched and strained against the sprocket teeth and then flung back, lashing with rebellious velocity, throwing Vody ten feet through the air. He landed with a harsh thud.

Following a barrage of curses, the soldiers gathered for another attempt. Vody took his place, and once again they hoisted the nearly 1000 pounds, charged forward and secured the track over the sprocket.

After tightening the track, the soldiers dispersed to their other duties. As Vody walked away, he felt a warm flow seeping down into his boot. He tugged up his pants leg to discover that when the track had flung back, an end connector had caught him below the knee, gouging out an inch of flesh. He considered the injury unfortunate, but incidental for a young, invincible soldier like himself.

Two hours later, he made his way up to the Oasis medical tent, a structure surrounded by a four foot high wall of sand bags. In one corner, cabinets and a refrigeration unit contained the essentials of medicine. The remaining tent area allowed for about 14 cots. Three of the cots were occupied by patients. Two of the soldiers suffered from malaria. In an effort to combat their high fevers, the men were stripped of their uniforms and doused with cold water.

The Doctor was perhaps 30, of average height and stocky. He had dark hair cut military short and brown eyes, sharp and intense. He indicated for Vody to sit on a stretcher that had been propped higher with ammunition boxes, and examined his leg, swabbed on disinfectant, numbed the area with several strategically placed shots, and stitched up the severed skin. The Doctor then wrapped the wound and instructed Vody to stay off his feet and keep the injury clean.

Vody followed the Doctor's orders for the first day, but by the next morning, he joined his tank crew for a series of missions. When they eventually returned, Vody limped back to the Oasis medical tent, his bandage having soaked up four days of sweat and dirt.

The Doctor cut off the filthy bandage, his irritation at the disregard for his instructions evident. Vody's leg was severely swollen, red and hot. The Doctor stuck the needle twice into the jagged edged wound and then proceeded with a ten inch tweezers and short, sharp scalpel to cut away the discolored flesh.

When Vody suggested that the shots were not working, the Doctor set down his tools, gave him a few more injections and then proceeded to again prod and tear away at the infected area, while reprimanding Vody for his complete neglect. The shots, intended to numb the pain, did not work nearly enough, but Vody kept quiet.

Once the injury had been rewrapped, Vody lowered himself from the stretcher, expecting to return to the Water Point. The Doctor objected. Vody argued. The Doctor advised him in a professional, commanding tone, with the inclusion of interjected adjectives, that if he again disobeyed his medical advice, the next time he showed up at the tent, his leg would need to be amputated.

Vody chose a cot in the far corner.

An occasional soldier entered the tent for minor ailments or injuries. On the third day of Vody's confinement, Mother's Day, a battalion size NVA force attacked the base.

The Doctor, the medics and the few patients evacuated to a nearby bunker. Vody grabbed up an M-16 rifle and a bandolier of bullets and positioned himself by the entrance.

Through the chaos of crashing mortars, rockets and the haze of dust, soldiers began returning, hauling the injured into the bunker and placing the stretchers on the ground where there was room. With the wounded, came reports of the VC within the wire. Three soldiers on duty in a listening post outside of the wire had been captured.

An understandable panic arose, a panic almost tangible, on the edge, ready to explode into something different for the sake of survival. . .a leap from logical and strategic to desperate, wild and cunning.

Vody leaned against the bunker's entrance, his finger on the trigger and his thumb against the safety. He glanced over the expanse of the base and considered his bunker location, wondering if better defense could be obtained elsewhere. If the enemy had already entered the perimeter, and if they found the bunker, then a cornered group of occupied medics, injured soldiers and the few men with weapons had no escape.

An advantageous position did not exist.

Explosions rumbled the ground, creating a deafening blur like constant thunder. In a scattered procession, soldiers continued approaching with the wounded. Vody peered into the distance, his vision trained to instantly recognize his own men, while scanning for the slightest shadow of deceiving motion.

Within the bunker, the medics worked with frantic pace, yet wounded soldiers waited, alarmed by the blood spreading over their uniforms. Some of these soldiers tried pulling themselves upward, their hands reaching to hold tight against the pain, warm red coloring their fingertips.

The Vietcong would be searching. The medics hastily gave shots of morphine to quiet these soldiers who yelled out with strangled cries of rapid breathing, mingled with fear and agony.

Pressed against the bunker entrance, Vody watched as the Doctor knelt beside a pudgy boy with blond hair. The Doctor ripped open the soldier's uniform and shined the olive drab flashlight at the wound. Trying to find the severed artery, he sank his hand into the boy's torn chest, the blood spurting up his wrist. He felt around, his shoulder slightly angled, and his expression blank with concentration as if listening for the answer.

He knew when death suddenly crept closer, stopping the slow heart beat of the boy. The Doctor's expression, for that instant, went rigid, recognizing the inevitable. He tilted the soldier's head back, his wet fingers smearing slick red onto the boy's pale face, and he blew into his mouth.

The Doctor was furiously focused, while the rhythm of the CPR became a crucial count of how much time he could allot to this soldier as other wounded arrived. He instinctively knew, from his experience in war, when he needed to comply with death, and yet each second only fueled his constant affront with failure.

Vody watched the soldier's limp body bounce with the Doctor's compressions. The boy's eyes stayed slightly open, with his face frozen in an unconscious daze.

With one final downward thrust, a check of the pulse, his uniform soaked with red, the Doctor ceased CPR. He quickly wiped the blood from his hands, glanced up and instructed the medics to move the body and bring him the next soldier. The Doctor's demeanor appeared calm, his tone efficient, as if the death of an unknown pudgy, blond haired boy held no consequence to him.

Two soldiers hoisted up the stretcher and carried the

dead boy over by the far end of the bunker entrance. Vody turned away, tightening his grip on the M-16. No prior belief of war could have properly described the watching of a soldier's death, or explained the numb oblivion necessary to survive in Nam.

Survival required that he forget the death of that soldier, even if the boy lay near him, his chest flooded with red, his blue eyes gazing glassy into nothing and his face smudged with his own blood.

The Doctor leaned over the next wounded soldier and scanned the injury with his flashlight. Despite the countless times that others had judged his aloof demeanor, he could not properly express his reasons. He had no time to explain how war necessitated the strict prioritizing of his capabilities. The war demanded that he save soldiers while other soldiers were destined to die, a contradiction to his training and belief.

Every soldier brought before him had friends who expected him to save that soldier. Every soldier brought before him had a family waiting. . .hoping that he would save their son, but he could not save the boys who were losing more blood than he could replace. He could not save the boys with shredded organs past repair. He could not fix the unfixable.

He had in the beginning, resisted resignation to defeat, demanding of himself to save every soldier, but in the end, boys died, and he needed to keep hidden the emotions not preferred of men in war. For the sake of the other soldiers, he knew he needed to appear confident and capable, despite his fear and doubt.

Like every soldier, he had learned that emotions skewed his skill and wasted precious time. Like every soldier, he had eventually learned that in war, death is neither generous with time nor sympathy. He had learned to accept loss as inevitable, but he had not yet discovered the secret for forgetting the faces of boys who died in front of him.

He did not need others' expectations. He, alone, held the strictest judgment of his own worth.

As the assault ended, the sky hummed with choppers, gun ships patrolling the area and dustoff choppers descending. The Doctor knelt amongst the wounded, stabilizing each soldier for transfer. Vody stood by the bunker entrance, near the dead, his finger on the trigger.

Such is the consequence of survival to watch again and again within the darkness of nightmares the images of war. Such is the consequence of survival to hear, years later, the slow, strangled suffering of boys. Such is the consequence of survival to remember, even with the tempering of time, the details of a soldier's death. In the outcome of war, no advantageous position exists.

The three soldiers captured and held as Prisoners Of War survived and returned home.

ONE SOLDIER

I want to give another Soldier's story that he cannot give, not because he died, but because he lived. I want to give this Soldier's story, because he is not alone in his torment, yet the torment began when he realized that he was alone. I did not witness the battle, but he told me what he remembered, and every soldier understands how death happened in Nam. His story needs to be known.

One night, mortars struck like thunderous, blazing steps across the blackness. Rockets ripped up the red dirt and blasted through piled sand bags. Soldiers who had been braced behind their M-60s, guarding the perimeter, were blown back, thrown hard against the ground, slashed by shrapnel.

The whisper of death began.

The Vietcong advanced, disguised in darkness, while the soldiers scrambled from their foxholes, shooting off flares, the green glow swaying the shade of images from below across the night's sky.

Keeping stride with the sergeant, the RTO repeated into the radio a request for backup, while ranking officers hurried amongst their men, giving orders that the young soldiers followed with trained obedience.

Explosions cracked, tossing soldiers like military trinkets, men landing on the ground clutching their shredded limbs, bones shattered and blood flooding through their uniforms.

This Soldier watched his friends fall in front of him, around him, next to him, while the medic darted between blasts to reach these injured men shaking from shock.

The Vietcong kept advancing nearer within the LZ. The RTO, crouching low, his voice raw, urged for reinforcements, while the explosions deafened him to the static of the radio.

Eventually, the medic ran out of morphine, and thus he knelt by his dying Brothers with only bandages, compassion and attempted promises. The wounded pleaded for something to lessen the pain, and when the medic told these boys that he had nothing left to give, some soldiers cried while gripping the medic's arm. Some soldiers called out to their families. Some soldiers simply closed their eyes.

The medic began choosing whom he could help, crawling from one soldier to the next while listening for gasps of breath, turning other soldiers over, only to find severed chests or helmets dripping with blood.

The surviving commanders kept directing their troops, but their orders got lost in the chaos. Soldiers with ashen faces and eyes like wild horses charged in darkness, while the Vietcong attacked like a thousand silver vipers, tightening death's chain.

There became a time in the midst of the battle when this Soldier was surrounded, outnumbered, his ammunition low. Men he knew like brothers were sprawled on the ground, pleading for help that he realized would never arrive. The medics were dead and the RTO was dead. This Soldier wanted to wrap his arms around his Brothers, but he needed to keep being a soldier, even as shock began to blur his thinking.

He stumbled over bodies, blood smudging his boots. He prayed to any protective Power who would listen as he fired his M-16 in bursts of rage, revenge and an unbearable grief.

He thought about the enemy's torture tactics. He thought about his family. He thought about the other soldiers' families. He felt death in front of him, around him, waiting for him.

Blasts showered down, scorching the dirt with flicks of flame and lighting the eyes of dead soldiers as they stared into the unknown. He no longer heard the voices of his Brothers, only the strangled groans of boys dying in the darkness.

This Soldier crawled over by his friends, and with a glance at their faces, snatched up their ammunition, ramming the clip into his M-16.

He tried to remember with detail what he had been taught in training. He understood that he had learned tactics for hand to hand combat, an array of defense strategies, but when had he learned how to die?

Mortar and rifle smoke floated over the camp in a heavy gray haze. Explosions echoed until the roar engulfed him. A bullet struck, jolting him backwards. He dropped his rifle. His hand drifted to the pain, and when he pulled his fingers away, his palm was wet and sticky. He tried to slow the gush of warm red and retrieve his rifle, but he staggered to his knees and then fell forward, his helmet cracking against his skull.

With dimming vision, he watched the Vietcong step amongst his friends, aiming their AK-47s downward. When the enemy heard a murmur or saw a soldier twitch, they flicked the aim of the barrel to the soldier's head and pulled the trigger.

The images blurred. The gun fire became little better than a fading echo, until a cold weariness lulled this Soldier into an emptiness.

He did not remember the end, or the next day when soldiers walked through the LZ, restraining their emotions as they hauled bodies to the trucks. He did not remember the soldiers walking past, believing him dead.

Months later, when this Soldier awoke from unconsciousness, he did not know what had happened until an officer told him that every other soldier had died. He alone survived. . .One Soldier.

This Soldier has kept this story for the hundreds of soldiers lost, not merely numbers but names of friends, sons, and brothers. He keeps for himself an unfounded guilt for having survived. He wonders why he didn't die on that night. At times, he wishes that he had died with the others, because what he yet hears and sees over and over and over again of that battle feels far worse than death.

I want to give this Soldier's story to honor him and those who died on that night. His story needs to be known. His story needs to be remembered.

WATCH TOWER

Specialist E-5, garbed in full gear, would whisk his way up the ladder with a 23 pound M-60 strapped over his shoulder, plus the weight of ammunition draped across his chest. On top of the watch tower, his helmet tipped slightly back, he would position himself for guard duty, keeping the hand crank radio within reasonable reach, while the tower spot light resurrected the twisting barbed rolls of concertina wire from the darkness.

He and I had been in training together. I ended up at the Tank Park, and he was assigned to the Motor Pool. Once in a while we crossed paths, because our barracks were in close proximity, and we would talk briefly before getting back to our work.

Specialist E-5 was a black soldier, over six feet, with a sinewy build, and a preference for wearing dark shades. Amongst the other soldiers, he usually worked alone, leaning over an engine, understanding the terrain of gears and electrical wires within military equipment far better than maneuvering through the jungle.

The change in him did not happen all at once, but imperceptibly like the slow sinking of a ship. He could not cope with war by the usual routes of resignation, determined endurance, or blatant, reckless behavior. He shook his head with weary despair when units went out on patrol and returned with fewer men. He stared blankly at the radio, as the panicked voice of a RTO could be heard pleading for reinforcements for his troop stranded under enemy fire, reinforcements that never arrived.

He listened, not because he wanted to know, but because to have walked away would have felt like abandoning his Brothers in their last hour. He found no redemption in the consequences of war, and within that hopelessness he began drowning.

On guard duty rotation, he again climbed the watch tower ladder, the M-60 pulling him back as he pulled himself upward. Again he would stand behind the wall of sand bags, peering into the blackness, watching explosions flicker and vanish within the jungle.

He knew more trucks would be driving past the Motor Pool, trucks piled with bodies, the rigid black bags shifting slightly as the trucks took the turn.

I don't know if he attended the memorials, but the church organ music could be heard wafting from the chapel in a slow, fading pulse. Almost every soldier had a belief of the beyond, but every soldier decided differently on how they would watch their friends die and yet keep faith in their God.

Each time I returned from a mission, Specialist E-5 had faded further from who he had been before. As the number of dead soldiers kept rising, he kept sinking, dragged down by the images that tore against decency.

His boots bearing down on each rung, he took his place in the watch tower, clutching the M-60 while perceiving the night with disdain. He did not want to die. He did not want to hear the church organ playing for more of his Brothers. He did not want to hear the grind of the trucks stacked with dead soldiers. The anguish followed him, because his innocence, his goodness, refused to forget the dead, but by dwelling on those who had died, he became caught in the tragedy.

About four months into my tour, I returned from a tank mission and found Specialist E-5 standing near the barracks, glancing into the distance, like he was watching something, but he wasn't watching anything. When I approached, his expression briefly hardened, as if trying to block the truth. He told me in a low voice, like we were surrounded by the enemy, that he hoped the sergeant could help him. His fingers were trembling as he rubbed his fist across his jaw, and he jammed his hand into his pocket.

He talked as if he needed to keep talking, or perhaps he needed someone to keep listening so that he could believe in hope, believe in the eventual escape. Then he trudged off, his eyes focused on the ground, as he meandered through the buildings.

Two weeks later, as Specialist E-5 stood quietly, a medic and a soldier from his barracks secured him in a straight jacket.

How does a soldier escape the torments of war? If he volunteered to serve his country, honor held him to his word. If he was drafted, he could not hide. If within battle he was seriously wounded, his injury became a heavier burden than the rucksack that he had hauled upon his back. If he intentionally shot himself, he was blamed. If he broke beneath the ruin of war, he was forsaken. If he survived his tour, the darkness followed him home. In the end, a soldier only escaped the war when the church organ played for him.

MILE HIGH

War cannot be written without agonizing images. Even the sharpest chosen words barely reach the depth of the desperation and fear that we heard, the pain and death that we watched, and the despair and suffering that we endured. Neither the passage of time nor the faded black and white photos of soldiers smiling takes away this truth.

Gibbs and I swore that we would never be taken alive. If on a tank run we were surrounded by the enemy and our ammunition nearly gone, we agreed that one of us would kill the other...a deed of mercy, and then use the last bullet on our self. Such decisions needed to be understood. We knew what happened to captives of low rank.

When we reached the end of the dirt road, Gibbs climbed from the VTR, and talked with the commanders of two other tanks. They talked for about 20 minutes, gesturing emphatically and looking at the expanse of the dense jungle.

When they finished their conversation, they walked over, and I slid from the top of the VTR.

According to intelligence, the VC had been amassing troops and weapons for an ambush on a small LZ in a place called Mile High. Outnumbered ten to one, the soldiers at that Landing Zone knew that if attacked, they had little chance. They knew about the nearby base that had recently been obliterated.

The four of us discussed the plan of going through the

jungle where the Vietcong could easily overrun us. The commanders told me and Gibbs that if we agreed with the plan and our tank got hit by the enemy's B-40 rocket, we had about ten seconds to get out of the VTR and into one of the gun tanks before that tank would turn and blow up our VTR. If we were wounded and could not escape in time...well, we would become part of the blast.

The commanders referred to our effort of bringing reinforcements to this LZ as a suicide mission. . .purely voluntary. Gibbs glanced at me. I nodded. We were those soldiers only hope.

One gun tank took the lead, having an extra man aboard as navigator, who had earlier mapped out the directions. Gibbs and I followed in our VTR, responsible for removing whatever trees the Vietcong had blown up onto the path. Another gun tank took last in line.

Our small convoy forged forward at about ten miles an hour, the tank engines thundering through the jungle, the tracks crushing and ripping the thick, wet vines and cramming between trees.

Gibbs sat above, manning the .50 caliber. He told me to put my seat all the way down, but I did not prefer the restricted observation range of the viewing ports. Instead I lowered the seat where I could yet scan above the hatch, with orders to drop down and lock up if we got hit.

With only a dim light breaking through the fanned leaves of the jungle trees, every shadow became the enemy bent on keeping us away. Within that vastness of green, we were the intruders.

Eventually, we reached the LZ, and the soldiers had an opening through the concertina wire awaiting our arrival. We drove through, and with the VTR, I dug trenches for the two gun tanks, deep inclines allowing the tanks to drive down the slope, fender level, with only the tanks' turrets above ground. I then excavated an area for our tank and drove down and shut off the engine. One gun tank was now stationed on either side of the perimeter, with our VTR finishing the defensive triangle.

Gibbs and I cleaned our M-16s. I then sat on the top of the tank and checked my .45, while Gibbs lugged up the box of extra ammo and rechecked the .50 caliber machine gun.

To the north, the jungle climbed a nearly vertical cliff, with trees that towered like titans. Around the LZ, a clearing of about 75 yards spanned beyond the perimeter. The strategically positioned grunts waited in their trenches, protected by the perimeter concertina wire, stationed trip flares and claymore mines.

We were set up, prepared for an attack. Gibbs took first watch. I stayed up as usual, talking with him and then had the second two hour guard duty.

During the night, a creature hit a trip wire, creating an orb of light, and every soldier was on full alert. Shot off flares floated down on parachutes, the yellow green flames spitting in the darkness, lighting the terrain in an altered glow.

Only with the sunlight, did the LZ soldiers lean back in their trenches, wiping the grime from their faces. Keeping close to the .50 caliber, I watched as two LRRP soldiers crawled from a trench. Without being detected, these two soldiers had crossed through the 75 yards from jungle into the LZ with only a scattering of brush for concealment.

These soldiers of the Long Range Reconnaissance Patrol were trained and gifted with the ability to become one with the earth, blending with the rhythm of the jungle. They lived on bugs, berries, roots. . .whatever they could find. They moved like spirits in their camouflaged uniforms, light on their boots, crouching low amongst the foliage, using hand signals for words, using intuition to feel the slightest shift of energy.

With their boonie hats obscuring their darkened faces, the two *Lurps*, with unreadable expressions, their rifles tilted against their shoulders and long, curved knives stuck through their belts, strode over by the other grunts. The conversation lasted but briefly, but the demeanor of that group of soldiers reflected their respect for each other. With smooth strides the recon patrol soldiers then went to report to the command bunker the location and number of the enemy.

A while later, they returned from headquarters, reached the edge of the perimeter and then disappeared like they had walked through a mystical door.

Days passed without an attack, the grunts dirty and tired in their trenches and us tankers alternating watch behind the guns. Although my senses were locked on the land, watching for the slightest indication of the enemy, I could not catch the covert route of the LRRP soldiers as they appeared and disappeared. These soldiers held an unexplainable instinct and ability, and I wanted to know those secrets that they knew.

Occasionally I would walk over by the grunts. They talked with an edge in their voices about things other than the probable fate of their LZ, but their attention never strayed from the wall of jungle.

On one particular day, I walked past the trench and noticed a soldier in his sleeping bag. He kept motionless, only blinking when sweat dripped from his hair and rolled into his eyes.

I asked the other soldiers about him. One of the guys answered, *snake*. I offered possible suggestions, but they had already considered those options. The soldier would simply have to wait until a few hours of intense sun prompted the snake to leave.

Apparently, during the night, the soldier had awoken when he felt the snake slide along his neck. Being strapped in the sleeping bag, he knew that he could not crawl out quick enough before the snake reeled forward with poison.

Without a defense, the boy had watched the snake slither past his vision and felt it coil alongside his ribs. He struggled to keep his breathing quiet, swallowing carefully with a parched throat, controlling the panic as the heat made his skin sting and his muscles twitch.

With the light of dawn, as other soldiers gathered their gear, this soldier, with an alarmed expression, kept motionless. The other soldiers, having quickly ascertained the predicament, quietly collected their weapons.

The trapped soldier knew his training, intelligence and M-16 were useless against the reptile breathing beside his ribs. He knew that within the jungle, the Vietcong were approaching, yet his fear of the enemy no longer held priority, while a more imminent threat lay within his sleeping bag.

The snake eventually became too hot and slithered away, and the soldier, with relief, joined his platoon in the trenches.

Day and night, Gibbs and I alternated watch on the VTR. The Lurps would reappear, giving their report on the enemy, and even though I tried to follow their exit, they would melt back into the jungle without detection. Over a week went past without an attack, and a few days later, the LRRP soldiers reported that the Vietcong were retreating.

The soldiers who completed their tours in Nam and returned home would never know the extent of the events, coincidences and individuals who played a part in their survival. Often times the best of courage and sacrifice occurred without notice, without praise. Soldiers acknowledged the unknown efforts of their Brothers by their own sacrifices, and in the end, they did not need to know the name of every soldier who once walked quietly upon their path, because it was enough to know that they had not walked alone.

KNIGHTS' TOUR

Seven minutes separated the two soldiers in the five ton bridge truck from the rest of their convoy. With the diesel engine rumbling in a low growl and exhaust howling through the pipe, the driver followed the narrow black paved road that sliced through the terrain from Pleiku to An Khe.

Craig Johnson, riding shotgun, scanned the wall of jungle on both sides, the butt of his rifle on the floor boards and the barrel gripped within his fist. He knew that if the Vietcong targeted their lone vehicle, he and the driver had no adequate defense.

The last sprinkling of the monsoon rains had blurred the windshield with murky slashes of dirt, and as the sun hovered over the horizon like a dimmed white sphere on a cold October morning, the driver noticed an approaching V-100. Keeping his speed steady and giving an occasional glance towards the rear view mirror, the driver watched as the Military Police vehicle gained ground.

Dale Moravec, the driver of the V-100, accelerated to 45 mph, hoping to catch a convoy which had left earlier for An Khe, his escort vehicle being crucial in securing the route. He had just recently turned 20. Only 54 days remained of his tour in Nam, and he held onto the belief that he would survive, return home and be able to accomplish the things that existed far away from war. The day felt good.

Alongside of Moravec sat a Vietnamese interpreter. A sergeant sat in the turret, operating the twin 60 machine guns, and also on top, but at the rear of the V-100, sat Radio Operator David Higgins. Trained as Combat Highway Military Police, Moravec, Higgins and the sergeant belonged to the *Roadrunners* of the 504th Battalion.

When a helicopter gun ship droned directly over, an uneasy energy drifted within the quiet. Higgins glanced up. Gun ships were usually not out so early, and neither his V-100 nor the convoy truck further in front should have been on the road alone.

Moravec gained position directly behind the truck and veered to pass, the back left wheel forced off the road, cutting over the dirt. As the V-100 swerved, Higgins braced himself for a revelation to the bleak premonition that had followed him that morning.

With a roar like a raging dragon, the earth rebelled, lifting the back of the V-100, clawing through the steel and wrenching off the wheel, shredding and melting the rubber as if tattered black cloth.

The force of the exploding anti-tank mine lifted and launched the four soldiers from the V-100. Soaring through the air with their legs and arms wide, they grappled for balance within the nothingness.

Events of Moravec's life clicked through his thoughts like the frames of a slow movie, and in desperation he implored of God not to let him die. Then he plummeted down, crashing onto the road, his right foot taking the force of the fall, and sending the impact up his leg and back. Momentum dragged him forward, and with every length, his body bashed against the ground, until he ended sprawled on the road, lost in the blackness of unconciousness.

Higgins flailed against the eerie weightlessness, metal shrapnel spinning along side of him, and then he felt himself falling, falling fast, adrenaline surging through him with the swift descent. He landed on his right arm, and then tumbled forward, the asphalt raking through his uniform.

The V-100 had shielded Johnson and the driver from the direct impact of the anti-tank mine, but the force of the explosion yet rammed against their bridge truck. Gripping the steering wheel, the driver struggled to keep on the road and out of the way of the seven ton V-100, which had flipped up onto its headlights and then slammed over onto its top, shearing off the twin 60s, while sliding alongside of their truck.

When the driver began slowing down, uncertain where the four injured soldiers had ended, Johnson told him to keep going. He expected an ambush to follow the explosion, knowing that the enemy buried road mines with the intention of halting an entire convoy.

The V-100 continued skidding for nearly 100 yards, the friction of metal grinding against asphalt, hissing sparks and finally tugging the vehicle to a halt. Johnson and the driver kept going until they had cleared another 50 yards further.

Only a quiet emptiness followed. Johnson waited, listened and then motioned to the driver. They grabbed their rifles and gear, and began walking along the edge of the road towards the accident.

David Higgins, having landed on his back, tried to understand what had happened. His feet and hands felt cold and heavy, the muscles limp. He strained his vision, frantically searching his perimeter for the other three V-100 soldiers and for a weapon, but he could not see the others and both his M-16 and M-79 had been flung far beyond his reach.

If the enemy ambushed, he was without a weapon and unable to move. Dire images conjured within his thoughts, and panic quickened his already erratic breathing. He did not want to die. He did not want to die without at least a fighting chance.

Craig Johnson and the driver approached, scanning the trees and keeping their rifles ready. One reality became undeniable. Death could be waiting on the path, and not only from the enemy. What they feared more than their own deaths, was finding their Brothers dead and seeing the expressions of young men who had struggled against pain and fear, and in the end lost.

They found the V-100 soldiers separated from each other, their uniforms blotched with red, and their legs and arms bent in distorted angles.

As the driver took one direction to check the further away soldiers, Johnson knelt by the interpreter. He sifted through the satchel strapped onto his leg, his hands shaking as he readied the bandage. He then wrapped the soldier's head wound, while glancing around at the emptiness of the road and the overturned V-100 seeping gasoline, the fumes permeating the air.

The jungle loomed dark and unpredictable. The four soldiers needed far more help than he and the driver could give. He decided that he would try getting to the radio beneath the V-100.

Seven miles ahead, Michael Bennett, of B Company 504th MP, *Roadrunners* Battalion, listened to the vague but intense chatter on his radio. No one of the convoy knew exactly what had happened on Highway 19, but Bennett caught the chopper pilot's radioed explanation: *explosion* and *need support*. The driver turned the jeep around, followed by two other Military Police jeeps, and Bennett, along with the eight other soldiers began back.

With the arrival of the three convoy vehicles, Johnson felt a rush of relief, knowing that the Military Police would be equipped with a radio and better medical capabilities prior to dustoff. He informed one of the men of what had happened, while the other soldiers secured the area. As the group of Military Police assessed the situation, Johnson and his driver walked back to their bridge truck.

Realizing that they would be driving the rest of the route alone, the driver accelerated the vehicle to maximum speed, as Craig Johnson scanned the wall of green, the barrel of his rifle gripped within his fist.

The cracks of AK-47s erupted suddenly from the jungle. The gunners in the jeeps swung their M-60s into position, rattling off rounds. The six other Military Police soldiers hit the ground, their M-16s on full auto, firing in short bursts.

Bennett could see Higgins lying 15 yards away as a constant barrage of bullets twanged against the road and ditches. Tipping his helmet back and taking a deep breath, he prepared himself to cross through the fire and reach his battalion Brother. The assault quickly escalated with B-40 rockets and mortars, trapping the nine MP soldiers and the four injured men in an all out enemy ambush.

Bennett's fingers tightened on his M-16, as his body braced to charge. He calculated the rate of the crashing mortars and the intensity of rifle fire against his determination to execute the 15 yards without getting killed. Urging himself forward, his boots dug into the dirt, he timed his advance, but his muscles froze, holding him down on his stomach. He fought against the animal instinct that owned him, would not release him. . .would not give his body the command to move.

Higgins stared into the dim sky, time eluding him as if he were watching the scene but from far away. He saw the gun ship swoop lower, the runners tilting for balance above him, the thumping blades sounding slow and lonely against the explosions.

When a deuce and a half pulled up, he watched as Special Forces soldiers jumped down from the back of the truck, and with adept strides fall into defensive formation, flanked along both sides of the road, their rifles and machine guns leveled on the jungle.

One of the Special Forces soldiers crawled over by Higgins and examined his injuries, focusing on the right arm already darkening with swelling. He slid one hand under the wrist and his other hand under the bicep, trying to lift evenly. Higgins winced as the elbow flopped uselessly in the center of shattered bones, and he shifted his glance.

The soldier's sleeve had a blue arrow patch with a gold sword, the hilt at the base with the blade rising vertically. Across the blade at 45 degree angles were three gold lightening bolts. Higgins knew that encounters with the Green Beret were rare, and his gratitude for their arrival did not need to be expressed with words.

He asked about the other three V-100 soldiers. The Green Beret spoke calmly, assuring him that the other men were alright. Higgins let that hope occupy his thoughts. The Green Beret had not said the word *dead*. He had not answered allusively. He had not kept quiet as if not wanting to answer. Higgins knew that perhaps he was being told what he needed to hear right then, but he trusted the Green

Beret, a soldier whom he would never forget.

Through the haze of rifle fire and mortar blasts, Bennett turned and saw the Special Forces soldier with Higgins. He knew that encounters with the Green Beret were rare, and he thankfully accepted that blessing for his Brothers.

Then Bennett heard a tank's tracks pounding in heavy sections against the road. He looked towards Higgins and then to the rapidly approaching tank and then back to Higgins. Having only the urgency of his thoughts, he tried to alert the driver.

Higgins watched as the 58 ton vehicle rolled towards him, and as the tank neared, he considered the unfortunate circumstance if the driver didn't see them. He alerted the Green Beret. The soldier was already watching, his expression tense, but he kept kneeling next to Higgins and holding his arm, with no intention of abandoning his position.

With only a few lengths between them, the tank driver, in one swift, smooth maneuver, spun, locking the right track and turned a 90 degree angle into the bush, the recoil of the main gun lifting the front of the tank.

The numbness began fading, and Higgins felt the pain of his injuries throbbing deep into his bones and muscles, striking nerves. The intensity gripped him, and he rocked back and forth, hoping to control the pain, while the Green Beret, yet holding his arm, patiently tried to convince him that he should keep still.

Even if he could understand the soldier's concern, Higgins could not stop. Only the pain existed, merciless and complete like an invisible dagger lashing through him. The pain pursued Higgins, and he defended himself by concentrating on the constant motion.

Moravec opened his eyes and saw a medic leaning over him. The soldier was talking, explaining that he was going to give him a shot of morphine and that a chopper was on its way. Moravec listened to a voice blurred by chaos, not fully comprehending what was real. His body felt like cold clay, twisted and without feeling. He wanted to know if the other three V-100 soldiers were alright, but the question was trapped in his inability to move or talk. The needle sunk into his backwards leg, and the blackness returned.

Propped on an elbow, Michael Bennett reloaded his M-16. The enemy ambush had been squelched with the arrival of the tank, but the dwindling bullets yet struck dangerously near and the mortars continued plummeting down in thunderous booms. The consequences of war had brought together the V-100 soldiers, the Military Police, the Green Berets and the tank driver. The energy of their unity became their shield.

The chopper pilot increased velocity as he entered the ambush site. Focused on a 20 foot by 20 foot area, he navigated the chopper down, the propeller blades creating swirling gusts, and the runners rocking into a horizontal line as he landed amid gunfire and explosions. The sergeant and the interpreter were loaded, and the chopper rose, the rotors drawing up air.

Five minutes later the second chopper cut through the haze, the pilot risking the precarious landing.

Two medics lifted Higgins onto the stretcher, and leaning low, hurried him onto the waiting chopper. Higgins felt the needle sink into his thigh as a soldier grabbed the frame of the stretcher and slid him next to Moravec.

Between the lulls of the morphine's effect, Moravec felt the sway of flying and glimpsed the blue sky drifting past.

He awoke at the 71st Evac on a stainless steel table with medics around him, talking in clipped phrases and working at a frantic pace.

The cold metal pressed against Moravec as a medic cut off his uniform and yanked away the red stained cloth from beneath him. He could not disregard the unnatural angle of his leg, the numbness of his body or that he was covered with blood.

He wanted a medic to tell him that he would be alright, but his thoughts seemed incidental and incoherent. He felt the slight tug of his foot and heard the gnawing of the blades as the scissors hacked through the nylon of his boot. He needed to believe that he would eventually return home, and with that hope, he asked the nurse if she would save his boots for him.

Elsewhere at the 71st Evac , a medic hoisted Higgins up by the shoulders. His right arm dropped limply, and an excruciating pain erupted as the medic tugged down his flak jacket in order to take x-rays. With another shot of morphine, time and reality drifted past.

The next day, the soldiers at the 71st listened as the enemy attacked from beyond the perimeter, the mortars falling nearer and nearer to the buildings. The medical staff rushed amongst the beds, helping soldiers onto the floor and throwing mattresses on top of those patients who could not be moved.

With a cast from his chest down to his feet, Moravec knew that his fate hinged on the precarious nature of war. A nurse placed pillows around his head for protection, and he and the other men lay quietly, trapped by their injuries, as approaching mortars shook the ground.

With his arm in a sling and a mattress thrown over him

because of his broken pelvis, Higgins yet heard the steady thwacking of an incoming chopper. A few minutes later, a pilot strode into the building as if oblivious to the explosions. Walking between the beds, the pilot scanned the soldiers' faces. When he found the particular soldier whom he was looking for, the two men talked like brothers. . .men who had struggled together and understood that in war, as soldiers found themselves stripped of everything, the spared life of a friend held profound significance.

The following day, an officer entered the Evac with another soldier of lower rank keeping stride. The officer glanced around the room and then raised his clipboard. He proceeded to call off names, his voice in succinct military tone, as he walked the aisles, watching for the intended soldiers to give indication. When the officer had exhausted that option, he continued down the rows, while the young soldier with him checked the bed charts.

Halting by one of the beds, the officer sharply stated the soldier's last name. With the hazy effects of morphine, Higgins heard his name but did not fully comprehend the situation that appeared to drift as if a slow, blurred dream. He did not reply...could not reply, because the morphine and the impact of his injuries kept dimming reality. The officer, noting Higgins' disoriented state, tossed a small black box onto the end of his bed and then proceeded onward. For the other soldiers on the list who were asleep, the officer's approach proved equally aloof.

For the men who were awake, the box was given with a brief affirmation of their courage. Some of the men, dazed with morphine, watched with listless expressions. Some of the men, who were simply trying to breathe steadily through their pain, kept their eyes closed, ignoring the visitors. Some of the soldiers took the hinged box and opened the cover slowly, as if it could explode. They looked at the Purple Heart, their thoughts lost in the images that had allotted them such a valiant acknowledgment, and then they snapped the box closed.

All of the soldiers of the 71st Evac deserved to be acknowledged with proper respect, and Higgins felt a sad disappointment because of the officer's approach in presenting these men with their Medals of Honor, but perhaps, this officer's own tour in Nam had dragged his hope towards such a dreary place that he could no longer retrieve enough thoughtful encouragement even for deserving soldiers. Perhaps he had watched too many of his own men die, and wanted to keep emotions locked away. Perhaps this officer simply could not find the strength for a task that entailed walking through a room of suffering and sacrifice that he knew could not be repaired by the mere presentation of a significant medal.

Again the effects of morphine tugged Higgins away, and when he awoke, he found that a nurse had placed his Purple Heart beside him. For Higgins, the honor reflected an emotional gratitude for every soldier doing what needed to be done for the sake of their Brothers.

When Dale Moravec awoke, he found a Purple Heart pinned onto his pillow, and felt thankful and fortunate that he and the three other soldiers of the V-100 had survived. He felt confident that his injuries could be repaired, and that he could eventually return to his battalion, however, the serious condition of his broken femur had drawn priority, and the continued morphine had cloaked the pain of his other injury. Only weeks later would a doctor at Camp Zama Hospital realize that Moravec's harsh impact with the road had also fractured his back.

Higgins awoke at the Cam Ranh Bay Hospital...every soldier within the room broken differently by war. He watched as a nurse approached one of the men. She sat on the edge of the soldier's bed and talked with him. Despite his pain, the soldier replied with politeness and appreciation. He was young. His face was scarred with red gashes from shrapnel. He had lost both of his arms. He had lost both of his legs.

This soldier's battle would not end with his return from Nam. The war had taken too much from him, and yet he shared his courage and light. Every soldier in that hospital honored his sacrifice with a quieter endurance of their own.

Higgins transferred next to the Air Force Hospital. The empty hours gave him time to think about the things of war that he had been trying to forget. He found his emotions colliding.

That evening, a nurse approached his bed with careful steps, her hands steadying a small round fish bowl that she held against her faded green fatigues. She was young, tall and slender. Her brown hair had been pulled back into a tail with a few loose strands slipping from behind her ear and brushing across her cheek. She walked with a confident grace and had a pretty smile, but her smile appeared to hide the sorrow that she allowed herself only when alone. She placed the bowl down on a table next to Higgins' bed and lightly touched his hand before going to the next soldier.

With the slight waves in the water, the florescent orange fish skirted around in frenzy, its nearly translucent fins swaying, and then lulled to a halt, peering contently through the glass.

Surrounded by suffering, David Higgins found refuge in

the quiet, calm of the fish. The nurse had given him a simple token, but with the gesture, she had without words, let him know that she understood how he felt lost between who he had been before Nam and who he had become. Her kindness gave him reason to believe that he and the other soldiers would eventually find a path home.

Time tends to delineate war into strategic tactics, notable battles, the comparison of fire power and the number of casualties. It would be easier to write about the Vietnam War with only such impersonal facts. It would be easier to simply acknowledge that soldiers survived battles, without knowing the fear of those soldiers, and the decisions expected of them. It would be easier to accept that soldiers simply returned home, without thinking about these young men returning from the war with missing limbs, scarred bodies and memories fraught with anguish. It would be easier to think only of the victories and honorable medals without the casualties. It would be easier to know the number of casualties without knowing the names. It would be easier to know the names without knowing the soldiers' ages. It would be easier to know the soldiers' ages without seeing their pictures. It would be easier not to remember the way soldiers sacrificed, suffered and died. It would be easier, but not the entire truth.

Psalm 23

I did not intend for this story to be written. While the details of other stories simply entered my thoughts, the details of this day always evaded me. I believed that I could not remember enough of what had happened in a valley of the Central Highlands on a road south of Kontum. There was no story, only fleeting images that I had tried to banish.

The detriments of watching death day after day while in Vietnam have blurred the past, but a few incidents of the war became lost intentionally.

I learned to forget certain things about my tour in Nam, except when the truth took me back during the night. I learned to not see some of the images, deliberately dulling the sharp edges. Once in awhile, I could even lose the worst of what happened, so that I could for a brief time forget.

If I could forget the images, I thought that I could then forget the pain, but the emotions could not be dimmed. Eventually I understood that I would never escape. Then I waited for the nightmares, because seeing the raw truth again and again was better than feeling a relentless anguish that I could not fully grapple with because of missing pieces. The nightmares have become swift, deep slashes that ease the pain like the numbness that fills a soldier when he has lost too much blood.

I did not intend for this story to be written.

Ten miles away, a group of soldiers, their tank broken down, stranded and low on ammunition, were waiting for us, because they knew that without our fire power and our ability to tow them back, they had little chance of surviving the night. Gibbs got behind the .50 caliber machine gun, while I drove. . .no helmet, no shirt, the warm air feeling cool, gusting against me.

With the new engine, I had removed the seals from the injector pumps and adjusted the governor to increase our RPMs to about 3000, knowing that we were near the verge of blowing up the engine, but I felt only the exhilaration of the ride.

In the Central Highlands, our tank surged with each climb, and upon the summits, we could see the expanse of the valleys below. The black road cut between the areas that had been sprayed with Agent Orange, burning the wall of green to a barren flat land except for a few abandoned bushes. Seventy five yards in, the jungle flourished on both sides, lush and thick and wild, with trees reaching the far heights of the sky. With the weight of the tank rolling swiftly down the slopes. . .I felt like I was flying.

We began the decline into a valley, when we saw a halted convoy, the lead Military Police vehicle having been hit, a tire blown off, causing the front fender to tilt against the ground. The infantry soldiers had evacuated the deuce and a half trucks, and were using the ditches for cover.

About 14 soldiers lay dead or wounded alongside of the road, beneath the continuing rifle fire but unprotected from the mortars being walked across the land.

Hidden within the jungle, one enemy mortar team was aiming at the convoy, and with our arrival, another team began trying to pace the mortars with the speed of our tank.

Explosions were erupting every 30 seconds, about 15 to 20 yards apart, plummeting down and ripping up the earth in murky funnels, showering down dirt.

While Gibbs fired into the tree line, I gauged where the next mortar would hit, knowing that the enemy had our tank rather accurately aligned. I swerved to the left, and a mortar struck to the right, rattling the bulk of the tank like a quake beneath our tracks. I swerved to the right, and another mortar landed slightly to our left, obscuring the path with heavy dust.

When we reached the convoy, my attention turned towards the soldiers sprawled alongside of the road. The mortars continued to fall, but the thought of running over any of those boys brought a dread not describable. Again and again, I turned the tank hard, the entirety of my training and ability focused on keeping the safety of the wounded and the honor of our dead.

Another mortar struck near the right, tossing a jeep. A soldier who had taken cover behind the vehicle got yanked off the ground. The force lifted him into the air, his knees slightly bent, feet dangling in the dark haze, with his head back as if resting on a wave of the explosion and his limp arms reaching wide like an angel waiting for the light.

He landed with a harsh thud, a crumpled figure in olive drab, blood seeping through his uniform.

Past the convoy, the mortars kept following our tank, but further and further off target, until Gibbs and I were far from range. I glanced back, wanting to turn around and offer fire support. I wanted to help the wounded. I wanted to know if the soldier had survived, because once we kept going, I would never know.

I only knew that I would forever remember the image of

that boy, lifted by the explosion, as if he were flying. . .but we needed to keep going, because there were those other soldiers, over the next rise, their tank broken down, stranded and low on ammunition, desperately waiting.

The tank surged with the climb and upon the summit I could see the expanse of the next valley, the black road cutting across the land and the jungle with trees lush and thick and green, reaching the far heights of the sky. I was driving fast, knowing I was near the verge of blowing up the engine, but I felt only the despair of war.

No doubt, details of that day have been lost, but the story that I thought I had forgotten. . .wanted to forget, was never about the details. This story is about the infantry soldiers who died on that road south of Kontum, the soldiers I could not help.

For the sake of my Nam Brothers, I have searched the past, *returning* time and time again to the trenches to find the details. I have listened in the darkness to the cracks of AK-47s and the agony of the wounded. I have walked in the monsoon rain, humped through the jungle and watched soldiers die.

For too long a time this story has teetered on a precarious edge. . .images that I had wanted to escape, but soldiers that I have wanted to honor. For those soldiers, I have *returned* to that valley on a road south of Kontum and remembered.

IN THE END

Why write about the Vietnam war. . .a brutal, faulty war that lasted too long and inevitably failed? Why write about a war that feels far away and forgotten?

Soldiers died.

Soldiers lived.

The soldiers deserve to be remembered.

War is dark, relentless, painful, but we were not the war. We were the soldiers who had struggled within that darkness and pain. . .not fathoming for what we were volunteering or what we were told to do for our country. We were boys ordered to be men.

When we returned home from Nam, wearing our less trodden uniforms, our composed military appearance proved an illusion draped over our battered bodies and ravaged emotions.

When we walked through the airport, unraveled by the confusion of panic, lowering our heads and reaching for our M-16s that had been taken away, we realized that we had not really escaped the war. The darkness and pain had followed us home, and we could already feel the war waiting to drag us back.

We returned from Vietnam changed, the traps of war defining our lives. While in Vietnam, we had resigned ourselves to dying, because acceptance of our own death made existence easier. When we did not die, we had already traded away our dreams.

When we returned, we planned no further than getting through each day without the Vietcong ambushing us. Every path became a terrain that we could not trust, as we stepped stealthily across the ground, watching for trip wires and buried mines.

We never stood with our backs to an entrance, because the black clad enemy was yet hunting us down, lurking in darkness until we turned our attention, and then they would attack, their AK-47s blazing. Our time in Vietnam conditioned us to be wild animals, surviving by instinct, endurance and cunning, and rules meant little to boys who believed that they would be dead before the end of a year.

When we returned, we were yet like wild animals, prepared to defend ourselves, pacing during the night, searching our perimeters, dedicated to the belief that our obligation and objective was to survive and help our Brothers survive.

No one else saw the shadows, and thus, they did not understand why we could not find worth in accomplishing the trivial things. Life lacked purpose.

During the night, dead soldiers yet visit us. We see their faces and hear their voices. Our lost Brothers visit us in desperation, wanting us to help them as they drown in the red, but we can do nothing to save our soldiers. . .just like in Nam, we could do nothing as our friends died.

We had returned home, but no one else noticed the war yanking us away, though we quickly learned to keep quiet about the things that had happened in Nam. Flashbacks became our own secret exiles, images twisting through our thoughts in agonizing accuracy. We tried to crush the truth and act as if we had never been in the war, but we could not stop being soldiers. How we were trained, what we saw, what we did in war could not be forgotten. We have tried.

We have tried to outrun the past in the roaring engines of our cycles, reckless speeds to escape the shadows, our POW ★ MIA flags flapping against the wind.

We have tried to lose our past in bottles that dull our memories and numb our emotions. We have tried to defend against our unfounded guilt with brash behavior or complicated, misunderstood silence. Some soldiers have kept the worst of war in a box of bullets stashed near enough to their gun.

We have tried, but the images take us back, boys casually holding rifles, boys whose pure faces have long ago faded but cannot be forgotten, and so we keep searching, searching to forget, searching to remember, trying to find our Brothers, trying to find peace.

The truths of war could not be changed, only compensated by the deeds of men both rebellious and brave, yet what is gained from war never compensates for what is lost.

War goes beyond the battles, the victories, and the number of casualties. War is about pain, fear, hopelessness, panic, resignation, resilience, pride, courage, camaraderie, survival, sacrifice. . .the deeper truths.

We walked relentless hours with the weight of our rucks and weapons. We lived in trenches, soaked by rain and scorched by heat. We never *really* slept.

We were challenged by jungle terrain, malaria, poisonous snakes, buried mines, trip wires, explosives, punji sticks, swamp waters and an overwhelming enemy. Those were only the tangible things.

We were also challenged by fear, doubt, loneliness,

anguish, desperation, despair, conscience, chaos and the certainty of death.

Physically, soldiers had to keep going. Emotionally, soldiers were given little exemption, although targeted at every turn, knowing that they must keep killing in order to survive, while watching each other die.

Soldiers cannot be blamed for hasty decisions while bullets shrilled past their helmets or for rebellious behavior in an effort to keep doing what needed to be done, or for guarding against the mirages of war. Soldiers cannot be blamed for wanting to live.

Why write about the Vietnam War. . .a war that feels far away and forgotten? The soldiers deserve to be remembered. The soldiers deserve to be remembered, because they watched out for each other even as bullets shrilled past their helmets. They persevered, even though exhausted and afraid. They kept their courage, even as their friends died. These boys deserve to be remembered and acknowledged, because while suffering the worst of life's trials, they found the strength to simply try.

POW ★ MIA
YOU ARE NOT FORGOTTEN